J. Rupert Kerry.

Lincoln Christian College

D1087346

Lincoln Christian College

THE HOUSEHOLD OF GOD

THE
HOUSEHOLD
OF GOD

*Lectures on the Nature
of the Church*

by

LESSLIE NEWBIGIN
Bishop in Madurai

SCM PRESS LTD
56 BLOOMSBURY STREET
LONDON

First published 1953
Reprinted - 1954

Made and printed in Great Britain by
Staples Printers Limited, at their Rochester, Kent, establishment

262.7
N53

To
MICHAEL HOLLIS
IN GRATITUDE AND
AFFECTION

31187

CONTENTS

PREFACE

THE Kerr Lectures given in Trinity College, Glasgow, during November 1952 are here printed as delivered, with minor verbal corrections. I must begin by expressing my gratitude to the Committee of the Kerr Lectureship for the honour they did me in inviting me to give these lectures. The decision to accept the invitation was prompted by the sense that, having had the privilege of sharing in the life and ministry of the Church of South India during the past five years, I was under an obligation to try to think systematically about what that experience had to teach; and that without the application of some such spur as the lectureship provided I was unlikely to do any systematic thinking about it. I have not attempted to cover all the field which may be included in the doctrine of the Church, but have deliberately restricted attention to the question which seems to me to be central in the present ecumenical debate, the question of the nature of the Church itself. The reader will find here no attempt to deal with the doctrines of the ministry and the sacraments or of the standard of faith. I have simply tried to make a contribution to the discussion of the question 'By what is the Church constituted?' The first chapter sketches the present context of the discussion and touches on the biblical meaning of the word 'Church'. The next three lectures examine the three answers to the central question, which may be roughly characterised as Protestant, Catholic and Pentecostal. The last two chapters argue that the Church is only to be understood in a perspective which is at once eschatological and missionary, the perspective of the end of the world and the ends of the earth.

I have included few references to the literature of the subject, partly because my knowledge of it is far less than it ought to be, and partly because in a work of such a limited character I found it difficult to relate my line of thinking at each point to the thought of those from whom I had learned by reading and discussion. I think my debt to many writers not named in the footnotes will be obvious; it would take a very long paragraph to acknowledge it fully.

A word must be said about one very large omission. I have said nothing about the Eastern Orthodox interpretation of the life in Christ. This would be unpardonable in anything that pretended to be a systematic treatise on the Church. I am quite sure that the recovery of the wholeness of the Church must depend heavily upon what the Orthodox have to teach us. The omission of this whole element from the present argument is simply due to the fact that my knowledge of the Eastern Church through reading and personal friendship is too slight to justify any attempt to speak of it in a book.

It is a great pleasure to acknowledge my debt of gratitude to those whose personal help has made it possible to prepare and deliver these lectures. The staff of Trinity College gave me freely their friendship and encouragement and made my visits to the College a pleasure not easily forgotten. The Foreign Mission Committee of the Church of Scotland made it possible for me to devote a good deal of my furlough to this work. The Rev. Professor William Manson of Edinburgh University and the Rev. Canon A. R. Vidler of Windsor were good enough to read through the typescript and to make many helpful suggestions. The Rev. Professor T. M. Torrance of Edinburgh University helped me in the early stages with books and suggestions for reading. Miss Helen Macnicol has also helped with criticism and advice and has kindly undertaken to read the proofs and prepare the index. Finally the Rev. Ronald Gregor Smith of the SCM Press has made several valuable criticisms and has been, as always, a most helpful and understanding publisher. To all of these I tender my hearty thanks. To the Church of South India I owe the richest experience that I have had of fellowship in God's people. I hope that these chapters may not be wholly unworthy of that experience. The usual author's royalties will go to the support of its work.

I have written what follows with the prayer that God may use it to help those who read it to 'apprehend with all the saints what is the breadth and length and height and depth' of the love of God, and to set forward among Christian people that peace and unity which are agreeable to His will.

LESSLIE NEWBIGIN
Bishop

I

INTRODUCTION

I

THE doctrine of the Church has come in recent years to occupy a central place in theological discussion. The reason for this is to be found in the interaction of several closely related factors, and it will be well at the outset to look briefly at these, since they provide the context for our discussion. I am going to refer to three such factors: the breakdown of Christendom, the missionary experience of the Churches in the lands outside of the old Christendom, and the rise of the modern ecumenical movement.

1. *The Breakdown of Christendom.* By this phrase I mean the dissolution—at first slow, but later more and more rapid—of the synthesis between the Gospel and the culture of the western part of the European peninsula of Asia, by which Christianity had become almost the folk-religion of Western Europe. That synthesis was the work of the thousand-year period during which the peoples of Western Europe, hemmed in by the power of Islam to east and south, had the Gospel wrought into the very stuff of their social and personal life, so that the whole population could be conceived of as the *corpus Christianum*. That conception is the background of all the Reformation theologies. They take it for granted. They are set not in a missionary situation but in this situation in which Christendom is taken for granted. This means that in their doctrines of the Church they are defining their position over against one another *within* the context of the *corpus Christianum*. They are not defining the Church as over against a pagan world. It is not necessary to point out how profoundly this affects the structure of their thinking.

The dissolution of the mediaeval synthesis and the transition to the world which we know today have brought the Church once again into direct touch with the non-Christian world in two ways, through the experience of foreign missions, and through the rise of anti-Christian movements within Christendom.

A study of the beginnings of the modern missionary movement shows how strongly this movement was still controlled by the old Christendom idea. Missions were conceived of as the extension of the frontiers of Christendom and the conveyance of the blessings of Christian civilisation to those who had hitherto been without them. The first converts shared these presuppositions, and were in most cases glad to adopt the culture of the missionaries along with their Gospel. But the rise of substantial Churches in Asia, Africa and the Pacific islands compelled re-thinking of these presuppositions. A distinction had to be drawn between the Gospel and western culture, and this in turn meant that the Church, as the body which—in whatever cultural environment —lives by the Gospel alone, had to be distinguished from the society in which it was set. In the first phase of missions, the colony of the *corpus Christianum* had been very clearly marked off as a totally distinct cultural community from the society round about it. The line of demarcation was very prominently represented by the high wall of a mission compound. But now the Church had outgrown the mission compound. Its members were scattered over city and countryside, sharing in a wider and wider variety of occupations with their non-Christian neighbours. Obviously a new kind of line had now to be drawn, a line dividing the Church from the world but not separating the Christian community from the local culture. The drawing of that line was the work of thousands of practically-minded men and women immersed in the daily care of the churches rather than of professional theologians. But its theological implications, which we shall consider in a moment, have been profound.

In the meantime, within the old Christendom the same issue was being forced upon the churches by the rise of non-Christian forces, at first more or less accepting the *mores* of Christendom while challenging its theology, but eventually launching a full-scale attack upon the whole ethical tradition of Western Europe and seeking to replace it by something totally different. In this situation Christian worship, teaching, and service could no longer be regarded as the religious activities of the whole community. The Church was compelled more and more to define itself both in theory and in practice as a body distinct from the community as a whole, and therefore to reflect upon its own nature. The present widespread discussion both in England and in Scotland of what has been called 'indiscriminate baptism' is one element in the present phase of that task.

But there is a further reason for the fact that the breakdown of Christendom has placed the doctrine of the Church in the centre of our thinking. One phase of that breakdown has been the dissolution of the ties which bound men and women to the natural communities of family, village, or working group, to which they had belonged. I do not need to labour this point, which is the constant refrain of the social diagnostician. Western European civilisation has witnessed a sort of atomising process, in which the individual is more and more set free from his natural setting in family and neighbourhood, and becomes a sort of replaceable unit in the social machine. His nearest neighbours may not even know his name. He is free to move from place to place, from job to job, from acquaintance to acquaintance, and—if he has attained a high degree of emancipation—from wife to wife. He is in every context a more and more anonymous and replaceable part, the perfect incarnation of the rationalist conception of man. Wherever western civilisation has spread in the past one hundred years it has carried this atomising process with it. Its characteristic product in Calcutta, Shanghai, or Johannesburg is the modern city into which myriads of human beings, loosened from their old ties in village or tribe or caste, like grains of sand fretted by water from an ancient block of sandstone, are ceaselessly churned around in the whirlpool of the city—anonymous, identical, replaceable units. In such a situation it is natural that men should long for some sort of real community, for men cannot be human without it. It is especially natural that Christians should reach out after that part of Christian doctrine which speaks of the true, God-given community, the Church of Jesus Christ. We have witnessed the appalling results of trying to go back to some sort of primitive collectivity based on the total control of the individual, down to the depths of his spirit, by an all-powerful group. Yet we know that we cannot condemn this solution to the problem of man's loneliness if we have no other to offer. It is natural that men should ask with a greater eagerness than ever before such questions as these: 'Is there in truth a family of God on earth to which I can belong, a place where all men can truly be at home? If so, where is it to be found, what are its marks, and how is it related to, and distinguished from, the known communities of family, nation and culture? What are its boundaries, its structure, its terms of membership? And how comes it that those who claim to be the spokesmen of that one holy fellowship are themselves at war with one another as to the fundamentals of its nature, and unable to agree to live together in unity and concord?' The breakdown of Christendom has forced such questions as these to the front. I think there is no more urgent theological task than to try to give them plain and credible answers.

2. *The Experience of the Christian Mission.* I have already referred to the fact that the contact of the Church with dominant non-Christian religious cultures outside of Europe raised practical questions about the relations of the Church to the world, and therefore about the nature of the Church itself. As a result of the effort to handle these practical issues, the question of the Church has come to dominate missionary thinking for the past two decades. It is necessary now to explain these statements more fully.

It is, I think, difficult for those who have lived only in Western Europe to feel the enormous importance of the fact that the Church is surrounded by a culture which is the product of Christianity. One needs to have had experience both of this, and of the situation of a Church in a non-Christian culture, to feel the difference. The Churches in most of the countries of Western Europe take it for granted that by far the greater part of the secular affairs of their members are conducted without any direct relationship to the Church. Education, medicine, art, music, agriculture, politics, economics, all are treated as separate spheres of life, and the Christian who plays his part in them does so as an individual, looking for guidance in them not to the Church but to acknowledged masters in each sphere who may or may not be Christians. It is no longer expected, nor would it be generally tolerated, that the Church should control these activities directly. Yet the fact that this whole body of secular culture has grown up within Christendom still profoundly affects its character. Christian ideas still have an enormous influence in the thinking and practice of those who take part in it. Individual Christians can make great contributions to it precisely because it is still so much shaped by its origin in a single Christian conception and practice of life. The Churches can, without immediate and obvious disaster, confine themselves to specifically 'religious' concerns, to the provision of opportunities for worship, religious teaching, and fellowship, knowing that their members will, in their secular/occupations, still have some real possibility of maintaining Christian standards of thought and practice. Thus the Churches tend to become loosely compacted fellowships within a wider semi-Christian culture, providing for only a small part of the total concerns of their members. Membership in a church may often involve only slight and relatively superficial contacts with other members, because the church is—for each member—only one among the many different associations to which he belongs.

I am well aware that this picture is only partially true, that all Churches in the West are not in the same position in this matter, and that many Christians deplore this development, are awake to its enormous dangers, and are seeking to reverse it and to find a deeper involvement of the Church in the 'secular' order. Yet the general picture is fair enough to provide a true contrast with the situation of the Church in the midst of an ancient non-Christian culture such as Hinduism. Let me now seek to sketch that situation in a few very rough strokes.

(i) In the first place, becoming a Christian in such a situation involves a radical break with the whole of the non-Christian culture. That culture may contain a vast amount of good, but it is determined by the dominant religious idea, and the convert therefore generally feels compelled to make a complete break with it. Later on, when he is securely established within the new community, he can assess the culture which he has left with a discriminating eye, seeking to preserve what is good. But that is only possible because he is now a member of a new community which is controlled by quite different principles. The majority of his contacts will now be with his fellow members in the church. He will look to them at every decisive point. His whole being is now enveloped in a new atmosphere, controlled by a new environment. He is, if one may put it so, not so much a man who has joined a new club as a child adopted into a new family. The church is the total environment of his life, rather than one among the circles in which he moves.

(ii) Looking now at the situation from the side of the Church rather than from that of the individual, we see that the Church going out into new territories has in most cases felt itself bound almost at once to involve itself in all kinds of service to the community—educational, medical, agricultural, industrial. It has felt compelled to try to demonstrate in these ways not merely a new pattern of personal behaviour within the pagan culture, but a new pattern of corporate activity extending beyond the strictly religious sphere. It may possibly be argued that this is a feature of post-Constantinian missionary work, and does not properly belong to the real business of the Christian mission. It is not necessary to argue the point here, for my concern is only to show that this, which has been a universal feature of missionary work in the modern era, has been one of the factors leading to a re-thinking of the doctrine of the Church.

(iii) Thirdly, the Church in a non-Christian cultural environment has to take seriously the business of discipline. That is a commonplace in the experience of every one of the younger Churches. It is necessary because, in the first place, the removal of the convert from the sphere of the traditional discipline of caste, community, or tribe, puts upon the Church the responsibility for seeing to it that this is replaced by a new kind of social discipline; and secondly, because without this the Church's witness to the non-Christian world becomes hopelessly compromised. It is often in this sphere that the sharpest necessity arises for the re-thinking of traditional attitudes derived from the Christendom background. Within Christendom one is familiar with two contrasted attitudes: on the one hand there is the attitude, typical of a national Church, which accepts a certain responsibility for the whole life of the community, but fails to make it clear that the Church is a separate community marked off from the world in order to save the world; on the other hand, and in opposition to this, there is the attitude of the gathered community—the body which is very conscious of being called out from the world, and from a merely nominal Christianity, but which yet can wash its hands completely of any responsibility for those of its members who fail to fulfil its conditions for membership. A missionary Church in a pagan land can take neither of these attitudes. On the one hand it must be a distinct body, separate from the pagan world around it. But, on the other hand, it cannot divest itself of responsibility for those whom it has uprooted from their ancient soil and transplanted into a totally new soil, or for their children. Perhaps this issue is less acute in some areas than in India. Certainly there the Church would be guilty of shocking irresponsibility if it did not accept some responsibility for all who, by baptism, have been removed from their ancient setting in the solidarity of caste and community, and brought into the community of Christ. In their baptism they have decisively broken the old ties of social discipline by which the common life was ordered, and if the Church does not make itself responsible for giving them a new and better kind of social discipline, it will stand condemned as an enemy of human well-being. But—as will at once be obvious—the effort to meet this need, to provide a type of discipline which is truly evangelical, which leads to Christian freedom and not to ecclesiastical tyranny, is one that raises the most difficult questions about the nature of the Church itself.

(iv) Fourthly, it is in this situation, as a new community set in, and yet separated from, the ancient religious cultures of the non-Christian lands, that the question of unity has become inescapable. Everything about such a missionary situation conspires to make Christian disunity an intolerable anomaly. Within the assumed unity of Christendom, the Churches could fall apart, increasingly leaving the main direction of the life of the world to secular forces, and concentrating on rival interpretations of the life in Christ, expressed in the form of religious fellowships which made a less and less total demand upon their members. But when they were thrust—for the first time for more than a thousand years—into a really missionary situation; when they were called to bear witness to one Lord and Saviour in the face of vast and ancient religious cultures which did not know Him; and when they began to see that to speak of Christ as Redeemer of the world was mere empty talk if the hard geographical implications of that phrase were not accepted: then it began to be clear that the division of the Church into rival and hostile bodies is something finally incompatible with the central verities of the Gospel. Much has been written in the last few years to bring to light again the profound connection at the very heart of the Gospel between mission and unity, and it is not necessary to repeat what has already been said. At the centre of the whole missionary enterprise stands Christ's abiding promise, 'I, if I be lifted up, will draw all men unto myself', and its goal is 'to sum up all things in Christ'. When the Church faces out towards the world it knows that it only exists as the first-fruits and the instrument of

B

that reconciling work of Christ, and that division within its own life is a violent contradiction of its own fundamental nature. His reconciling work is one, and we cannot be His ambassadors reconciling the world to God, if we have not ourselves been willing to be reconciled to one another. It is the result of this deep connection at the heart of the Gospel itself that Churches which—within Christendom—had accepted their disunity as a matter of course, found that when they were placed in a missionary situation their disunity was an intolerable scandal. Out of this new missionary experience arose those forces by which the Churches were drawn from isolation into comity, from comity into co-operation, and—in some areas at least—from co-operation into organic union.

And that leads us to the third factor in the context of our discussion—the rise of the ecumenical movement.

3. *The Ecumenical Movement.* The ecumenical movement has been a by-product of the missionary movement, arising out of the missionary experience of the Churches outside of the old Christendom, and enormously reinforced by the experience of Churches within Christendom which have found themselves here also in a missionary situation face to face with new paganisms. It is important to bear this fact in mind, for the ecumenical movement will become fatally corrupted if it does not remain true to its missionary origins. The very name ought to be a safeguard, were it remembered that in the New Testament *oikumene* never means the world-wide Church but always the whole inhabited earth to which the Church is sent. There is a real danger at the present time of a false sort of ecumenism, an attempt to find consolation amid the wreckage of the old Christendom in the vision of a new and wider Christendom, yet without the acceptance of the hard demands of missionary obedience. The attractions of this broad and comfortable blind alley must be resisted. There can be no true ecumenical movement except that which is missionary through and through, for there can be no true doctrine of the Church which is not held, so to say, in the tension of urgent obedience between the Saviour and the world He came to save. The fact that the World Council of Churches and the International Missionary Council, linked as they are in the closest association, are still two separate bodies, is a reminder of the fact that a thoroughly missionary conception of the nature of

the Church has not yet been wrought into the ordinary thinking of the Churches.

The decisive feature of the present stage of the ecumenical movement is the formation of the World Council of Churches. The implications of this event are only slowly being realised in the Council itself and in its member Churches. At Amsterdam the member Churches made this statement about what they had done: 'We have covenanted with one another in constituting this World Council of Churches. We intend to stay together. We call upon Christian congregations everywhere to endorse and fulfil this covenant in their relations one with another. In thankfulness to God we commit the future to Him.' These words indicate a very far-reaching change in the relationship of the Churches with one another. The ecumenical movement is no longer to be a matter for individuals or groups, nor is it to be concerned only with limited objectives. The Churches have bound themselves to one another in the sight of God and of the whole congregation of the faithful. Not all the implications of that act could be clearly discerned at the time. The same Assembly confessed, in thanking God for unity which the ecumenical movement had helped them to recognise: 'We acknowledge that (God) is powerfully at work amongst us, to lead us to goals which we but dimly discern. We do not fully understand some of the things He has already done amongst us, or their implications on our familiar ways.'[1] Reflection among the Churches as to what those implications were raised searching questions. In this covenant the member Churches had in some sense recognised one another as Churches. In what sense? Had they recognised one another as 'the Church' in the New Testament sense, and—if so—had they agreed to lay aside their own distinctive doctrines about what constitutes the essence of the Church, or to treat them as of merely secondary importance? If not, how could they treat as Churches bodies lacking elements which, upon their own view, are essential to the Church? These questions soon clamoured for an official answer.

Two years after the Amsterdam Assembly, the Council's Central Committee issued in 1950 at Toronto an extremely precise and carefully balanced statement of what the implications of membership were. This made it clear that membership did *not* imply that a member Church was obliged to treat the other

[1] Amsterdam Section I Report, para. VI.

member Churches as in the full sense Churches, or to regard its own doctrine of the Church as merely relative, or to accept any particular view as to the visible form of the Church's unity. Positively the statement listed the following assumptions as underlying the formation of the Council, and implied in membership. All recognise that Christ is the one Head of His Body, the Church, and that the Church is therefore one; each member Church recognises that the Church Universal exists *in some sense* beyond its own boundaries, that the question '*In what sense?*' is a subject for common study and conversation, and that this recognition of elements of the true Church in other Churches makes such mutual conversation obligatory; all recognise that they ought to seek together to learn from Christ what witness they should bear together in the world, to live together in mutual helpfulness, and to enter into spiritual relationships with each other to the building up of the Body of Christ. One may summarise the situation as this document states it by saying that the World Council of Churches gives institutional embodiment to the conviction that the Church ought to be one, while remaining neutral as to the proper form of that unity. It thus provides a place in which very diverse views as to the unity which the Church ought to have can confront one another in fruitful conversation. There are those who hold that the divinely willed form of the Church's unity already exists in their own communion (whether in assent to doctrines as formulated in a particular confession, or in acceptance of a particular historic order) and who therefore cannot regard bodies outside their own communion as, in the full sense, Churches. There are others who, holding a different view of the divine will for the Church, can accept as true Churches bodies of a very wide variety of types of doctrine and order. All of these are invited to become members of the Council and are assured that they are not thereby required to modify their views. The Council is a place where they can all meet and engage in fruitful converse.

And yet, of course, it is more than a meeting-place, a mere forum for discussion. When the Churches at Amsterdam spoke of 'covenanting together' they did not use empty words. Something came into existence there which had not existed before, a mutual commitment, leading to a new sort of unity in witness and action. The World Council exists, and acts more and more effectively in many spheres—in witness, service, the edification of the Body of Christ. This is a new fact, a new reality. And it exists because the member Churches have been unable to refuse to recognise one another as Christ's people. 'We are divided from one another,' said the Amsterdam Assembly, 'But Christ has made us His own, and He is not divided.' Whatever their doctrines of the Church, the member Churches could not refuse to make that momentous statement, and they cannot refuse to accept its implication, which is that their togetherness in the Council is—in some sense—a togetherness in Christ. No one who has taken any part in the ecumenical movement can doubt this: its unity is a unity in Christ. The World Council is not a mere neutral meeting-place for differing views of the Church: it has itself a churchly character.

It follows from this that, while we must accept the statement of the Toronto document that the World Council is *in intention* neutral on the question of the form of the Church's unity, we cannot agree that it is neutral *in fact*, for it is itself a form of that unity. And, if the Council be regarded as anything other than a transitory phase of the journey from disunity to unity, it is the *wrong* form. In saying this I am, of course, abandoning any pretence at speaking from a position of neutrality among the conflicting ecclesiologies with which we have to deal. I cannot so speak, for I believe that the divinely willed form of the Church's unity is at least this, a visible company in every place of all who confess Jesus as Lord, abiding together in the Apostles' teaching and fellowship, the breaking of bread and the prayers. Its foci are the word, the sacraments, and the apostolic ministry. Its form is the visible fellowship, not of those whom we choose out to be our friends, but of those whom God has actually given to us as our neighbours. It is therefore simply humanity in every place re-created in Christ. It is the place where *all* men can be made one because all are made nothing, where one new humanity in Christ is being daily renewed because the old man in *every* man is being brought to crucifixion through word, baptism and supper. Its unity is universal because it is local and congregational. Believing this, I am bound to believe that all conceptions of reunion in terms of federation are vain. They leave the heart of the problem—which is the daily life of men and women in their neighbourhood—untouched. They demand no death and resurrection as the price of unity. They leave each sect free to enjoy its own particular sort of spirituality, merely tying them all together at the centre in a bond which does not vitally and costingly involve every member in every part of his daily life. They envisage a sort of unity whose foci are not the word and sacraments of the Gospel in the setting of the local congregation, but the conference table and the committee room. They do not grapple with the fact, which any serious reading of the New Testament must surely make inescapable, that to speak of a plurality of Churches (in the sense of 'denominations'), is strictly absurd; that we can only do so in so far as we have ceased to understand by the word 'Church' what the New Testament means by it; that our ecclesiologies are, in the Pauline sense, carnal (I Cor. 3: 3-4). The disastrous error of the idea of federation is that it offers us reunion without repentance.

I am not wishing to assert that the World Council is a federal union of Churches. That is made clear by the Toronto Statement, and by the fact that the member Churches are not committed to intercommunion. Yet, in so far as it is an embodiment of Christian unity, it is a federal form of embodiment. And precisely because it is much more than a merely neutral meeting-place, because in it a real common life in the Holy Spirit takes place, because it is the locus of much that is most fruitful and precious in the life of Christendom today, because it is the increasingly effective organ of co-operation among Churches for all sorts of service and witness to the world, there is a real danger of our forgetting that the World Council only has a right to exist as a means to something further, as a stage on the way from disunity to unity; and that if it comes to be regarded as itself the proper form of the Church's unity in Christ, it will have become committed to a disastrous error. I believe that membership in the World Council is indeed the way that God has opened up in our time by which the Churches may move from disunity to unity, and that to refuse this way would be to refuse God's call. But it is the way, not the end, and if it comes to be regarded as the end it must be condemned as the wrong end. We have to recognise that the present situation is critical; that the Faith and Order discussions do not at the present moment seem to be leading to any adequate move forward in the direction of organic reunion; and that a very large number of Christians seem to be content to regard our present level of co-operation as sufficient. In other words, there is a real danger that the World Council, while proclaiming itself neutral as regards the form of the Church's unity, should in fact come to be accepted as the organ of a sort of federal union. There can be no doubt that very many Protestants[1] who ardently support the work of the Council do so with this underlying idea; they take seriously the fact that the Churches have, in some sense, accepted one another as Churches, and have covenanted together in the Council; and they are hurt and irritated by the refusal of Catholics to take what seems the next step—complete intercommunion among the member Churches. There are doubtless many who would regard such intercommunion as a step towards organic unity, but the evidence seems to me clear that a vast number would regard it not as a step towards organic unity, but as a substitute for it. The present position of the English Free Churches is an example of the evidence I refer to. In other words, federation is apparently accepted as an adequate goal. In this situation I think that the Catholics may be provisionally justified in their intransigence, that in refusing intercommunion on these terms they are perhaps, in the only way possible to them at the moment, maintaining their witness to the Scriptural truth about the nature of the Church which might otherwise be hopelessly compromised.

But the Catholics also are in a dilemma. For in sharing in the ecumenical movement they have become involved in a situation for which their traditional theology has no place. The Catholic rightly believes that it is of the nature of the Church to be one visible fellowship, and if he is serious he must believe that his own Church is that fellowship. He cannot, then, treat other separated bodies of Christians as Churches. Yet in the World Council he has found himself compelled to recognise them as, in some sense, Churches, and therefore to join with them in a binding covenant. But his own traditional theological language can provide him with no categories to justify what he has done, and he will constantly appear to others as insincere or inconsistent. He maintains, for instance, that episcopacy is essential to the

[1] It will be obvious that here, as frequently throughout these lectures, I am using the two words 'Protestant' and 'Catholic' in a very loose sense to describe the two major points of view represented in the present ecumenical conversation, and that the word 'Catholic' is not here being used as it is in the Creeds.

Church. That can only mean that where a body has no bishops it is no Church; that if it regards itself as a Church it is suffering from delusion; and that the only proper exercise of Christian charity towards its members is to deliver them from this delusion, and to bring them out of a pseudo-Church into the true Church. He repudiates that deduction because in the ecumenical movement he has come to know as a sheer fact that Christ is present in the other Churches. He cannot deny it without feeling that he is guilty of sinning against the Holy Ghost. The logical conclusion would then seem to be that he should correct the statement 'Episcopacy is essential to the Church' to 'Episcopacy is very valuable to the Church'. But that he cannot do without destroying his whole theological position. The Catholic is stuck in a logically impossible position. Yet by sticking to it he is defending a vital Christian truth which would otherwise apparently go by default.

The result is the stalemate with which we are painfully familiar. As an organ of co-operation and conversation, the World Council of Churches goes from strength to strength. But the visible reunion of the Churches makes little progress, and indeed denominational positions tend to harden. Thus the Council, instead of being something essentially transitional, tends to be regarded by many as the sufficient form of Christian unity. Its ecclesiological neutrality is in danger of becoming a screen for ecclesiological federalism. I have already said that I believe that this would be disastrous. Yet there is no way of avoiding that disaster except by finding some way of breaking through the theological impasse in regard to the doctrine of the Church. It is this actual situation in the relations of the Churches that gives its urgency to the subject I have chosen for these lectures.

II

Having said so much about the context of our discussion, let me say a word about the standpoint from which it will be conducted. I have already made it clear that I can make no pretence to neutrality. I can only speak from the place where I serve, which is in the ministry of the Church of South India. Standing in that place, I have very definite views as to the divinely intended form of the Church's visible unity. I have already indicated what they are. But perhaps the most important thing about the Constitution of that Church is the explicit confession that the Church is not what it ought to be. I should like to quote here some sentences from the statement prepared by the Church of South India for the Lund Conference: 'Probably no Church is as static as its fundamental documents suggest, but the Church of South India has the idea of development written into its very constitution. That constitution is explicitly a starting point; it does not pretend to be a final resting place. It was written by three Churches still divided from one another, as a sufficient starting point for the adventure of unity, and in the faith that truth would be more clearly seen in unity than in separation. It confesses its own partial and tentative character by acknowledging that the final aim is "the union in the Universal Church of all who acknowledge the Name of Christ" and it claims to be tested by the principle that every such local scheme of union "should express locally the principle of the great catholic unity of the Body of Christ" (Const. II. 2). Very obviously in these words the Church of South India confesses that it is not yet the Church in the full sense which the word "Church" ought to have. It confesses itself to be on the road, and it makes a claim to be on the right road, but it does not pretend to have arrived.'

If there is any single constructive feature in these lectures it will simply be the attempt to draw out what is involved in that statement. The Church is the pilgrim people of God. It is on the move —hastening to the ends of the earth to beseech all men to be reconciled to God, and hastening to the end of time to meet its Lord who will gather all into one. Therefore the nature of the Church is never to be finally defined in static terms, but only in terms of that to which it is going. It cannot be understood rightly except in a perspective which is at once missionary and eschatological, and only in that perspective can the deadlock of our present ecumenical debate be resolved. But—and this is of vital importance—it will be a solution in which theory and practice are inseparably related, not one which can be satisfactorily stated in terms of theory alone. There is a way of bringing the eschatological perspective to bear upon our present perplexities which relieves them at no cost to ourselves, which allows us to rest content with them because in the age to come they will disappear. That is a radically false eschatology. The whole meaning of this present age between Christ's coming and His coming again is that in it the powers of the age to come are at work now to draw all men into one in Christ. When the Church ceases to be one, or ceases to be missionary, it contradicts its own nature. Yet the Church is not to be defined by what it is, but by that End to which it moves, the power of which now works in the Church, the power of the Holy Spirit who is the earnest of the inheritance still to be revealed. To say that the deadlock in the ecumenical debate will be resolved in a perspective which is missionary and eschatological is not true unless it is understood that that perspective means a new obedience to, and a new possession by, the Holy Spirit. It is a perspective inseparable from action, and that action must be both in the direction of mission and in that of unity, for these are but two aspects of the one work of the Spirit.

III

Having spoken about context and standpoint, I must proceed to say something by way of definition. We are to be speaking about the Church, and it is necessary at the outset to say that this means a society of human beings, which—so far as those still living in the flesh are concerned—is a visible community among the other human communities. The question, 'What are its boundaries?', is part of the question we have to discuss, but just for that reason it is important to make clear that we are speaking of a society which *has* discernible boundaries. We are not speaking of an abstract noun, or of an invisible platonic idea. It is true that the Church includes those who, having died in faith, are now beyond our sight, but await with us the final day of judgment, resurrection and victory. We are not called upon to determine among them who are and who are not of the Church. They are in God's hands. But in respect of those now living in the flesh that responsibility is given to us. We are called upon to recognise and join ourselves to God's visible congregation here on earth. This congregation is truly known only to faith, because it is constituted in and by the Holy Spirit. But it is a visible congregation. As Schmidt says (in the article in Kittel's Dictionary to which I shall refer several times[1]), it is 'precisely as visible and temporal as the Christian man'. The point is so important that

[1] *The Church*, K. L. Schmidt. Tr. J. R. Coates.

we must devote some attention to it before closing this introductory lecture.

The whole core of biblical history is the story of the calling of a visible community to be God's own people, His royal priesthood on earth, the bearer of His light to the nations. Israel is, in one sense, simply one of the petty tribes of the Semitic world. But Israel—the same Israel—is also the people of God's own possession. In spite of all Israel's apostasy, Israel is His, for His gifts and calling are without repentance. This little tribe, and no other, is God's royal priesthood, His holy nation. And the same is true in the New Testament. There is an actual, visible, earthly company which is addressed as 'the people of God', the 'Body of Christ'. It is surely a fact of inexhaustible significance that what our Lord left behind Him was not a book, nor a creed, nor a system of thought, nor a rule of life, but a visible community. I think that we Protestants cannot too often reflect on that fact. He committed the entire work of salvation to that community. It was not that a community gathered round an idea, so that the idea was primary and the community secondary. It was that a community called together by the deliberate choice of the Lord Himself, and re-created in Him, gradually sought—and is seeking—to make explicit who He is and what He has done. The actual community is primary: the understanding of what it is comes second. The Church does not depend for its existence upon *our* understanding of it or faith in it. It first of all exists as a visible fact called into being by the Lord Himself, and our understanding of that fact is subsequent and secondary. This actual visible community, a company of men and women with ascertainable names and addresses, is the Church of God. It was present on the day of Pentecost, and the Lord added to it day by day those that were being saved.

The phrase Church or congregation or assembly of God (*ecclesia theou*), and the thing itself, are both carried over from the old dispensation. Schmidt shows in the article referred to that the essential meaning of the word depends upon the fact that *theou* always follows—expressed or understood. The word *ecclesia* by itself tells us nothing more than the English words 'meeting' or 'gathering'. We require to know who called the meeting, or who attended it. Here we are dealing with the Church or congregation of God. It derives its character not from its membership but from its Head, not from those who join it but from Him who calls it into being. It is God's gathering. And this explains the fact that, as Schmidt says, the singular and the plural can be used promiscuously and interchangeably, as they are in Acts and the Epistles, and both with the genitive *theou*. You can speak of God's gathering in Ephesus, of God's gathering in Smyrna, or of God's gatherings in Asia. This does not mean that the Church of Asia is made up of a number of local churches, or that the local churches are, so to say, subordinate 'branches' of the Church regarded as a whole. It means that God is gathering His own, alike in Ephesus and in Smyrna and in all Asia. 'Congregation of God' is equally the proper title for a small group meeting in a house, and for the whole world-wide family. This is because the real character of it is determined by the fact that God is gathering it. This may remind us of Christ's word, 'Where two or three are gathered together (the root being the same as in the word, Synagogue) in my Name, there am I in the midst of them' (Matt. 18. 20).

There is an analogy here with the use of the word 'Kingdom'. In the New Testament the phrase *basileia tou theou* means primarily the presence and action of the kingly power of God. The operative word—so to say—is *theou*. But in loose speech the word Kingdom has been used alone, as though it denoted some sphere or order of things which could be thought of in itself. The situation is similar, says Schmidt, with regard to the word *ecclesia*. The operative word is *theou* or *Christou*. It is the church or congregation which God is gathering in every place. It is God's Church and its whole character derives from that fact. The moment you begin to think of it as a thing in itself, you go astray. The God whose gathering it is may never, even for temporary purposes of thought or argument, be excluded from the picture. But at the same time it is a real gathering. God is really working. Therefore there is a real congregation. It is these people here whom He has gathered, and this is the Church of God.

In contradiction to this, the idea of the invisible Church, in its popular use, derives its main attraction—unless I am much mistaken—from the fact that each of us can determine its membership as he will. It is *our* ideal Church, containing the people whom we—in our present stage of spiritual development—would regard as fit members. And obviously the Church—so regarded—is a mere appendage to our own spirituality. It is not the Church of the Bible, but a mere idea which may take as many different and incongruous visible embodiments as there are varieties of human spirituality. The congregation of God is something quite different. It is the company of people whom it has pleased God to call into the fellowship of His Son. Its members are chosen by Him, not by us, and we have to accept them whether we like them or not. It is not a segregation but a congregation, and the power by which it is constituted is the divine love which loves even the unlovely and reaches out to save all men. There is, of course, a very important truth in the idea of the invisible Church: that which constitutes the Church is invisible, for it is nothing less than the work of God's Holy Spirit. But the Church itself is the visible company of those who have been called by Him into the fellowship of His Son. The great Pauline words about the Church as the Body of Christ, the Bride of Christ, the Temple of God, are addressed to the actual visible and sinful congregations in Corinth and in Asia Minor, and indeed are spoken precisely in connection with the urgent need to correct the manifold sins and disorders which the Apostle found in them.

The idea of the invisible Church must be examined more fully later. It derives its main force from the obvious fact that the visible Church is full of things which are utterly opposed to the will of God as it is revealed in Jesus. But Luther, who employed this concept in his polemic against Rome, also pointed the way to the truth in the light of which the problem of sin in the Church is to be interpreted when he insisted that justification by faith is the article by which the Church stands or falls. The problem of how an unholy concourse of sinful men and women can be in truth the Body of Christ is the same as the problem of how a sinful man can at the same time be accepted as a child of God. *Simul justus et peccator* applies to the Church as to the Christian. It seems to me that our present situation arises precisely from the fact that this fundamental insight which the Reformers applied to the position of the Christian man was not followed through in its application to the nature of the Christian Church, and this is one of the clues which we shall seek to follow in the present course of lectures. As Schmidt says in the phrase already quoted: The Christian community is precisely as visible as the Christian man.

But the acceptance of this truth leaves vast issues unsettled. If we agree that the Church on earth is the visible body of those whom God has called into the fellowship of His Son, we have to ask—where is that body to be found? We know where it was on the day of Pentecost. It was there in Jerusalem. But where is it today? By what signs or works can a body rightly claim today to be the Church of God? We are all agreed that the Church is constituted by God's atoning acts in Christ Jesus—His incarnation, life, death, resurrection, ascension, His session at God's right hand and the gift of the Spirit. But how are we of the subsequent generations made participants in that atonement? *What is the manner of our ingrafting into Christ?* That is the real question with which we have to deal.

I think that there are three main answers to these questions.

The first answer is, briefly, that we are incorporated in Christ by hearing and believing the Gospel. The second is that we are incorporated by sacramental participation in the life of the historically continuous Church. The third is that we are incorporated by receiving and abiding in the Holy Spirit.

The moment one has stated these three positions in this bald way, it is at once apparent that they are far from being mutually exclusive, that very few Christians would deny the truth of any of them, and that there is an infinite variety of combinations of and approximations to these three positions. Nevertheless I think that we can best approach our problem by isolating these three positions. Classical Protestantism, especially in its Lutheran form, of course ascribes an immense value to the sacraments. But the major emphasis is upon faith, and faith comes by hearing, and therefore the pulpit dominates the rest of the ecclesiastical furniture. It also knows and speaks of the work of the Holy Spirit but does so with reserve. It is shy of enthusiasm, and is reluctant to give a large place to the claims of 'spiritual experience'. Catholicism honours preaching and acknowledges the necessity of faith, but it finds the centre of religious life rather in the sacrament than in the sermon. It acknowledges a real operation of the Holy Spirit sanctifying the believer, but gives the decisive place rather to the continuous sacramental order of the Church. The third type—for which it is difficult to find a single inclusive name—acknowledges and values preaching and the sacraments, but judges them by their experienced effects, and is not interested in the question of historical continuity. All these three answers to the question can obviously make effective appeal to Scripture in support of the truth for which they contend. It will be our aim in the succeeding lectures to look in turn at each of them, its basis in Scripture and in the nature of the Gospel, and—in a very cursory way—at some of the light which the history of the Church has shed upon it. We shall also try to show the distortions which have resulted from taking any one of these answers as alone the clue to the Church's nature. In the two concluding lectures we shall try to consider the nature of the Church in the light of the fact that it is a community *in via*, on its way to the ends of the earth and to the end of time.

II

THE CONGREGATION OF
THE FAITHFUL

The view of the Church which I have put first has a certain natural primacy. The words with which, according to St. Mark, our Lord opened His public ministry were an invitation to believe. 'Jesus came into Galilee, preaching the gospel of God, and saying, "The time is fulfilled, and the kingdom of God is at hand: repent ye, and believe in the gospel." ' The beginning of His ministry is the announcement of good news, and the summoning of hearers to repent and believe. It is hardly necessary to give instances from the Gospels of this demand for faith. When asked what are the works of God, Jesus replies, according to St. John's Gospel, 'This is the work of God, that ye believe on him whom he hath sent,' and according to the same Gospel, to believe on Him is to have everlasting life. To believe is the condition of sharing now in the benefits of His mighty works of healing and cleansing. In the Acts, Christians are referred to simply as those who have believed. 'Believe on the Lord Jesus and thou shalt be saved' is the apostles' word to the Philippian jailor, and might be taken as a summary statement of their word to all. It is unnecessary to multiply instances, but it is important constantly to bear in mind that when the New Testament speaks of our relationship to Christ, it is the words 'believe' and 'faith' which are used at almost every essential point.

I

Special attention must however be given to the arguments which centred round the circumcision controversy. It is quite clear that, not only for St. Paul, but for the whole Church, this controversy raised issues fundamental to the Church's being. It could not be otherwise. The more one thinks about this whole episode in the life of the young Church, the more one is amazed at the revolutionary courage of the apostles, and their complete reliance upon the guidance of the Holy Spirit even when He led them far away from any track that God's people had trodden before. Consider the words of the Lord in Genesis, with all the force they must have had for a faithful Hebrew of the first century: 'This is my covenant, which ye shall keep, between me and you and thy seed after thee; every male among you shall be circumcised. . . . It shall be a token of a covenant betwixt me and you. . . . And the uncircumcised male who is not circumcised in the flesh of his foreskin, that soul shall be cut off from his people; he hath broken my covenant' (Gen. 17. 10, 11, 14). That token had been the mark of the covenant people throughout its history. The blood of martyrs had been shed freely to defend it. The Lord Himself had undergone circumcision, and by no single word had He suggested its abrogation. He had re-written many of the precepts of the Mosaic law, but the law of circumcision never. By what authority could His apostles dare to touch this constitutive sacrament of God's people, which He Himself had left untouched?

The whole answer, in one phrase, is—'on the authority of the manifest acts of the Holy Spirit'. The whole substance of the matter is contained in the brief and simple speech of Peter to the apostles and elders at Jerusalem as reported in Acts 15: 'Brethren, ye know how that a good while ago God made choice among you, that by my mouth the Gentiles should hear the word of the gospel, and believe. And God, which knoweth the heart, bare them witness, giving them the Holy Ghost, even as he did unto us; and he made no distinction between us and them, cleansing their hearts by faith. Now therefore why tempt ye God, that ye should put a yoke upon the neck of the disciples, which neither our fathers nor we were able to bear? But we believe that we shall be saved through the grace of the Lord Jesus, in like manner as they' (Acts 15. 7–11). According to the record in Acts, it was this statement, supplemented by the reports of the actual evidences of God's work among the Gentiles, that reduced the circumcision party to silence. Let us examine it somewhat closely.

1. St. Peter reminds them of what had happened at Caesarea. God by whose sovereign election Abraham was called out from his land and people to become the father of the faithful, by whom the apostles themselves were chosen to be witnesses of Christ, had likewise chosen Peter to bring the Gospel to the household

c

of Cornelius. He had prepared Cornelius and his household for the apostle's coming, and had given them the gift of faith in the Gospel preached to them by Peter. These were all God's saving acts as surely as His acts in calling Abraham. His mysterious choice always goes before our hearing or speaking. He chose us before the foundation of the world, and though what has happened may seem new and strange to us, we have to recognise that it is of God's sovereign will that it has happened.

2. This is no piece of abstract speculation. God has set His own seal upon His deed, provided His own proper witness in the person of the Holy Spirit. What happened in Cornelius' house was nothing doubtful or debatable. The Holy Spirit came upon that company as surely as upon the apostles at Pentecost. You cannot accept one event as the act of the living God, and treat the other as something else. God has given His Holy Spirit to the Gentiles, and not only in Cornelius' house, but—as brothers Paul and Barnabas will testify—in Cyprus, Pisidia, Galatia. To borrow a phrase from a later, but equally controversial document, 'God has bestowed His grace with undistinguishing regard'[1] upon them and us alike.

3. God has cleansed their hearts by faith, so that they are no longer to be treated as 'sinners of the Gentiles', as polluted pagans. They are to be received as God's holy people. The pollution of the Gentile is essentially—as Paul shows in the first chapter of Romans—God's judgment upon his unbelief. And conversely, faith cleanses the heart—or rather, God cleanses the heart by faith.

4. In the face of these facts, for us to lay upon the Gentiles the intolerable burden of the Mosaic law would be to tempt God. Tempting God is the precise opposite of faith. Faith is a complete founding of the whole man upon what God has said and done, upon His self-revelation. Tempting God means trying to get more assurance than God has given. God has called these Gentiles into the fellowship of His Son by the way of faith. For us to lay upon them the burden of the law will be to fly in the face of God, to contradict His way of working.

5. Whether for us or for them, there is only one assurance of salvation: 'We believe that we shall be saved through the grace

---

[1] *South India Basis of Union*, p. 2.

of the Lord Jesus.' God's way of salvation is by grace through faith.

It will be noted that there is no specific mention of circumcision in this statement. The circumcision party had asserted 'that it was needful to circumcise (the Gentile converts) and to charge them to keep the law of Moses'. Peter's speech deals with the law in general rather than with circumcision in particular, and it is clear from James' summing up, and from the encyclical which issued from the conference, that the question before the conference was in the form, 'How much of the burden of the law shall we lay upon the Gentile believers?' This is also true of the arguments of Paul on the circumcision controversy. He does not deal with circumcision in isolation as a rite of initiation into the covenant people. He deals with it, so to say, as the first and crucial instalment of works-righteousness. 'I testify again,' he says, 'to every man that receiveth circumcision, that he is a debtor to do the whole law.' We may imagine, though we have no direct evidence for it, that Paul's judaising opponents urged the necessity of circumcision as the guarantee of a place in God's covenant people. With the Old Testament as the only Bible of the Church this appeal must have had almost overwhelming force. If this is so, one may take it that both this brief speech of Peter and the arguments of Paul, go to the root of the question of circumcision in particular, as of the question of law in general, by showing that the two belong necessarily together, and are both parts of man's attempt to re-insure himself before God. For the believer, who has received the Holy Spirit and whose heart God has cleansed by faith, recourse to them would be tempting God. God's way of salvation is by grace through faith. He has marked the road by manifest signs. For man to seek more assurance than God has given is simply to abandon the road He has provided. The real issue is works versus faith, and circumcision, though it is the occasion of the controversy, is only incidental to the matter at issue.

But obviously this statement raises very difficult questions. What is the relation of this new work of God to His former works? Is the old covenant completely abrogated by the new? And if so, in what sense can the Church regard itself still as God's Israel? Has God, as it were, terminated His covenant with Israel and entered upon a new covenant with mankind upon completely new terms? Is Israel's calling now only a matter of increasingly remote history? Obviously that is not how the apostolic Church interpreted the situation. It unhesitatingly regarded itself as the Israel of God, it used the books of the old covenant as its Bible, and took to itself their promises and warnings. It regarded Gentile Christians as wild slips grafted into the stem of the good olive. All this implies a fundamental continuity with the old Israel. But the abandonment of circumcision implies a most drastic discontinuity. How, then, are continuity and discontinuity related? In what sense did Christ reconstitute the people of God? To what extent did the new covenant in His blood make void the principles of the old?

At the outset we must dispose of two wrong answers to our question. In the first place, the reason for discontinuing circumcision was not that it had been replaced by another equivalent rite. A great amount has been written in recent years to prove that there is a simple correspondence between circumcision in the old covenant and either baptism or confirmation (or both together) in the new. In spite of all that has been brought to light by these recent discussions, it remains true that the tremendous struggle about circumcision was not a struggle about two alternative rites of initiation into the people of God. It was a struggle about the fundamental principles upon which that people is constituted. In St. Paul's writings circumcision is contrasted with faith (Gal. 5. 6; Rom. 4. 10–12); it is spoken of as of the flesh, in contrast to that which is of the Spirit (Gal. 6. 13; Eph. 2. 11; Phil. 3. 3), as the outward in contrast to the inward (Rom. 2. 28–29). It is never contrasted with baptism as the old with the new. It is repeatedly said that in Christ neither is circumcision anything nor uncircumcision, because in Him there is a new creation, a new humanity. Only in one passage is circumcision brought into close proximity with baptism, and since this passage is constantly quoted in this connection we must refer to it. 'In Christ,' says Paul to the Colossians, 'ye were also circumcised with a circumcision not made with hands, in the putting off of the body of the flesh, in the circumcision of Christ; having been buried with him in baptism wherein ye were also raised with him through faith in the working of God, who raised him from the dead' (Col. 2. 11–12). 'A circumcision not made with hands' plainly does not mean baptism, for baptism is as much 'made with hands' as circumcision is. Nor is there any serious doubt as to what the phrase does mean. In the light of similar references in Ephesians (2. 11), Romans (2. 28–29) and Philippians (3. 2–3), and of the use of the phrase in contrasting the old temple with the new (Mark 14. 58; Acts 7. 48 and 17. 24; II Cor. 5. 1), there can be no doubt that it refers to that work of the Spirit of God Himself upon the heart, to which the prophets of the old dispensation had looked forward, and which had been granted in the new, the seal of the Spirit, the circumcision of the heart. The same contrast is being drawn here as elsewhere in St. Paul's writings between a circumcision which is merely in the flesh (what he elsewhere calls 'concision') and the circumcision of the heart which is the work of God's own Spirit. That true circumcision has been made possible to us by the death of Christ wherein He put off from Himself the flesh and all its powers (Col. 2. 15); it is sacramentally mediated to us in baptism, and appropriated by faith. If the point of the passage were the replacement of one rite by another, it is inconceivable that the phrase 'a circumcision not made with hands' should have been used. The new covenant also has its rites; of that we shall speak in a minute. But the true contrast drawn here as elsewhere is not of circumcision with baptism, but of circumcision in the flesh made by hands, with circumcision of the heart—the work of the Holy Spirit. This passage is in line with the rest of the Pauline references. And even if this interpretation could be disputed, there remains one fact which is—I submit—enough by itself to upset the equation 'Circumcision in the Old Covenant = Baptism in the New.' It is simply this, that in all the terrible heat of the conflict about whether or not circumcision should be demanded of the Gentile converts, this equation is never hinted at either in Acts, or in Galatians or Romans. Arguments from silence are sometimes precarious, but I submit that this one is unassailable. In the epistle to the Galatians we see the apostle in an agony of anxiety for his converts, seeking to lay hold upon every argument and every appeal which could convince them of the peril in which they stood. But we never hear him use the one argument which—upon the view which we are criticising—would have been decisive. We never hear him say, or come anywhere near to saying, 'You do not need to be circumcised because you have been baptised.' Nor is there a hint of this argument in the reports of the conference at Jerusalem. I find it quite impossible to believe that the apostle would have left unused the one argument which would have been—on this view—final. I think we may say that this, negative, statement is as certain as anything can be, that circumcision was not discarded because it had been replaced in the new dispensation by another rite. That surely is one negative point of real value in taking our bearings. But a second—equally important—is this. The reason for abandoning circumcision is not that it is an outward sign, and that the new covenant has no need of outward signs. That also is a common view, and to those who hold it it seems self-evident. 'The old covenant,' it is said, 'was a matter of external rites and ordinances: the new covenant is spiritual, written in the heart, and has no need of outward signs.' It is certainly true that the new covenant is spiritual, its laws written in the heart (Jer. 31. 33). But it does not, on that account, dispense with outward signs. The passage we have just discussed is a reminder of the fact that Paul takes it for granted that the seal of the Spirit, received in faith, is sacramentally mediated in baptism. In the next section we shall have to consider the place of baptism and the Lord's Supper in our incorporation in Christ, and there is no need to anticipate here. It is sufficient to remind ourselves that the reason for discarding circumcision was not that the new covenant dispensed with outward signs altogether. The new covenant certainly has its outward signs.

Negatively, then, we must say the abandonment of circumcision was due neither to the fact that another rite was substituted for it, nor to the fact that the new covenant had no need of outward rites. Positively I think we must say that the crucial terms in the argument by which it was resolved that Gentile converts should not be circumcised were the terms 'faith' and 'Holy Spirit'. That is certainly true of Peter's speech as we have seen. It is because God has cleansed the heart of Gentile believers by faith, and because He has given them the Holy Spirit, that the burden of the law is not to be imposed on them. And circumcision is—as I have said—treated as the first instalment of the burden of the law. But if that is so, wherein lies the continuity of the new Israel with the old? And what are, in fact, the ultimate principles by which God's people is defined and constituted?

To answer these questions we turn in the first place to St. Paul's most sustained arguments on the subject in the Epistles to the

Galatians and the Romans. In Galatians, after vindicating the claim that he had his gospel not from men but from God, and that his work among the Gentiles was done in perfect concord with the work of the Jerusalem apostles among the Jews (1. 1–2. 10), Paul plunges straight into the question by referring to his clash with Peter at Antioch on the subject of the Jewish food regulations. He immediately presses home the exclusive alternatives, righteousness by the works of the law and righteousness by faith. We infer that Peter, yielding to the pressure of Jewish opinion, was trying to get the best of both worlds—both the righteousness of faith and the righteousness that comes by the law. But Paul's logic is relentless: if we ought to keep the Jewish food laws, then to break them is sin. But your breaking of them so as to have fellowship with Gentiles was the result of your faith in Christ. Therefore Christ is a minister of sin. And you, who now try to build up again what—as a believer—you pulled down, are convicted as a transgressor. These two things are absolutely mutually exclusive. If you try to supplement faith righteousness by works righteousness you make Christ a minister of sin. The application to the circumcision issue is so obvious that Paul does not explicitly make it. He bursts forth into one of his utterly characteristic passages describing the life in Christ, crucified with Him, risen with Him, a life lived in faith—'the faith which is in the Son of God, who loved me, and gave himself up for me'. The life in Christ is altogether one of faith answering grace. To add to it the works of the law is to make grace void: 'for if righteousness is through the law, then Christ died for nought' (2. 11–21).

The same absolute dichotomy—either law or faith—is further pressed home in the next chapter. First, like Peter at the Jerusalem conference, he appeals to the acknowledged fact that it was by 'the hearing of faith' that the Spirit and all His works were made theirs (3. 1–5). Then, he goes back behind the Mosaic law, behind even the institution of circumcision, to the verse which tells us that Abraham was accepted as righteous on the ground of his faith in the divine promise. Therefore the true son of Abraham is he who founds upon faith, and he who founds upon the law is under the curse which God pronounced upon all who do not keep the whole law. Law and faith are incompatibles. But Christ has accepted for us the curse of the law that we might inherit the blessing of Abraham and receive—through faith—the promise of the Spirit (6–14). Those who are members in Christ are 'the seed' to whom the promise was made. And the law—given later—cannot annul the promise (15–18). The law is not contrary to God's promise but it serves the purpose of shutting up every way to God except the way of faith. Law cannot itself give life, but it can drive us to Christ. 'But now,' he says, 'you Galatians are all, by faith and baptism, members of Christ, the true seed of Abraham (19–29). Since you have been freed from this prison-house and made sons of God through reception of the Spirit of His Son, how can you turn back again to prison-routine?' (4. 1–11). In a passage of great tenderness he reminds them of their former love to him, and of his renewed travail for them that Christ may be formed in them, and then—using the allegory of Ishmael and Isaac—again seeks to convince them of the absolute incompatibility of law and grace. In a phrase of special solemnity he testifies to them that everyone of them who receives circumcision is 'severed from Christ'. He is no longer a member in the 'new man' who is Abraham's seed, for he is seeking justification by law. But of that true seed, he says, 'We through the Spirit by faith wait for the hope of righteousness. For in Christ Jesus neither circumcision availeth anything, nor uncircumcision, but faith working through love' (5. 2–12). The same key words are here again—the Spirit and faith. The new man in Christ is constituted from the divine side by the gift of the Spirit, and from the human side by faith. In Christ we 'wait for the hope of righteousness': our status is not that of those who have a righteousness of their own and are thereby acceptable to God; it is that of those who look to Him, wait for Him, rest on His promises as Abraham did, and who have received from Him a share in the Holy Spirit who is the earnest of all that God has laid up for us. What marks us as members in Christ is not circumcision nor uncircumcision but 'faith working through love', and this is the same as to say, as he does later, that the essential thing is not circumcision or uncircumcision but a new creation. Faith works through love because faith lays hold on God's love, opens up the channel through which God's love flows out and back through all Christ's members. To be in Christ is to be part of a new creation wherein the Spirit rules and brings forth His characteristic fruit. In the remainder of the epistle Paul describes these fruits, in their absolute contrast to the works of the flesh—the new creation in contrast to the old (5. 13–6. 10). Finally in the autograph post-script he brings the whole of his personal force to bear upon the effort to show them the absolute contrast between the two spheres —flesh and spirit, old creation and new creation. The demand for circumcision belongs to the world of the flesh. It is prompted by a desire to evade the scandal of the Cross, by which every fleshly glory is put to shame. The man in Christ can glory in nothing save in the Cross of Christ, in whom and with whom the Christian has died to the old creation that he may live in the new (6. 11 to end).

From the foregoing summary it is clear that the apostle resisted the demand for the circumcision of Gentile converts as involving an absolute severance from Christ, and that this resistance was based upon the conviction that the demand involved an attempt to supplement the righteousness which is by faith with the righteousness of the law. I think we can set out the essential points in the following way:

1. There are two spheres in which human life may be lived· The first is the sphere of law, wherein man hopes to win accept-ance with God by his obedience to God's law. In fact this sphere is under God's curse. It is the sphere of the flesh. The second is the sphere of grace, wherein man rests his whole hope of accept-ance with God upon God's revealed grace in Christ. This is the sphere wherein God's Spirit rules. We enter this sphere by hearing the Gospel, laying hold of it by faith and baptism, and receiving the Spirit.

2. These spheres are absolutely exclusive of one another. There is no possibility of any combination or compromise between them. If you try to supplement grace by works you have aban-doned grace.

3. This does not mean that the law is contrary to God's purpose. On the contrary, by the law God purposes to block up every other way except the way of grace and faith; to drive us to Christ. But having been set free in Christ we cannot return again to the bondage of the law.

4. The demand for the circumcision of the Gentiles involves acceptance of the whole sphere of law, with its unlimited obliga-tion, its confidence in the flesh, and its curse. Therefore for the Gentile Christian to be circumcised will mean being severed from Christ.

In the light of these basic convictions as they are expressed by the apostle in the heat of a mortal struggle for the souls of his own children in Christ, let us turn to the longer and more elaborate treatment of the same themes in the first eleven chapters of the Epistle to the Romans. He deals here not with an immediate crisis in his pastoral ministry, but with the wider issues raised by the relation of Gentile to Jewish fellow-members in the Body of Christ. From the point of view of our present enquiry we want especially to see how he relates a universal Gospel available to all believers to the concrete and distinct historic body of Israel, and how far and in what sense the Church is to be regarded as the new Israel, the continuation of that historic body.

The main theme of the epistle is announced clearly at the outset. The Gospel is the power of God to all who *believe*, for in it is revealed 'a righteousness of God by faith'—as the Scripture says, 'The righteous shall live by faith.' The righteousness of God by faith—that is to be the subject (1. 16-18). But the background of righteousness is wrath, for the righteous judge punishes evil and will finally judge the secrets of all men—circumcised or uncircumcised (1. 18-2. 16). In this final judgment circumcision will count for nothing; only he who has actually kept the law will be approved, whether he be circumcised or uncircumcised. True circumcision is not outward and visible but inward and spiritual (2. 17-29). Are we, in that case, left with a purely spiritual religion from which all outward ordinances have been dissolved away? Is it nothing to be a Jew, to belong to the visible *ecclesia*? On the contrary it is a plain matter of fact that God gave His revelation to the Jews. Then are we to conclude that because some who belong to the visible *ecclesia* are unfaithful, God's covenant is made void? No—God's faithfulness to His covenant is, so to say, thrown into relief by our unfaithfulness. Then shall we continue to do evil, that God's faithfulness may be the more commended? No—that idea is utterly incompatible with the truth that God will finally judge the world (3. 1-8). We shall deal with this later, but meanwhile the plain fact is that *all* men, inside or outside of the Church, have sinned. No one, Christian or pagan, has any chance of acceptance before God on the basis of his own fulfilment of God's law (9-20). But now there is revealed to us a righteousness of God which is not by law but by faith, a free justification available to all alike, through the redemption wrought in Christ 'whom God set forth, a propitiation through faith, by his blood'. By this all boasting is excluded, Jew and Gentile are alike justified by faith, and the law is not annulled but established (21–31).

But we must return to the problem of the old *ecclesia*. What was Abraham's real standing before God? Did God adopt the principle of works in dealing with him? No, the principle of faith. He accepted him solely on the ground of his faith, and he gave him circumcision to be the seal of that acceptance, so that he should be the father of all believers—whether circumcised or not (4. 1–12). God's promise to Abraham and his seed is addressed not to those who build on the law, but to those who, like Abraham, hope against hope, and believe the promises of God who is able to raise the dead, and who calls the things that are not as though they were (13–25).

So then it is through faith that we enjoy all the privileges of incorporation in Christ, we rejoice in hope, and God's love is shed abroad in our hearts through the Holy Spirit (5. 1–11). These two spheres stand over against one another; the old man— Adam, the new man—Christ. In the former sphere man's sin brings forth condemnation and death: in the latter, God's free gift of pardoning grace brings justification and life. Law does not rescue us from the former sphere, but has the effect of aggravating the rule of sin and making its real character apparent (12–21). Again the question is raised: Since we are not under the law but under free grace, shall we continue cheerfully to sin? Such a question has no meaning if you understand what has happened. In his death and resurrection Christ carried the old humanity down to the grave and rose in the glory of the new humanity. All we who are baptised have been made sharers in that death and resurrection. We are no longer members in the body of sin, but united with the risen Christ. By our obedience to the Gospel teaching we have become free from the bondage of sin and made servants of God enjoying His free gift of eternal life (6. 1–23). Death cancels even the most binding of connections, that of marriage. By your membership in the crucified Christ you have been divorced from law and married to Christ (7. 1–6). Not that the law is sinful; it is holy: but sin uses it as the instrument to get its deadly grip on me. Only Christ can deliver me from that grip (7–25).

But God has, through Christ, done what law could not do. He has made us free, heirs of the life which law promised but could not give, sharers in His own Spirit by whom we know ourselves to be God's children (8. 1–17). We suffer with Him in hope of His final victory. We know that all things are in His hand, that we are His own elect people, and that nothing can pluck us out of His hand (18–39).

But again we ask, what are we to say of the old *ecclesia*, Israel after the flesh, to whom God gave *everything*, His whole revelation of Himself culminating in the gift of Christ Himself (9. 1–5)? First we must say that God has not broken His promises—for His promise was not to the children of the flesh (all who could claim natural descent from Abraham) but to the children of the promise, those whom God has chosen beforehand (6–13). It is plain from history that God does choose some and hardens the hearts of others (14–18). He has this freedom as our Creator (19–24), and He has freedom to call strangers to be His own people and to execute judgment on His own people, leaving only a remnant (25–29). The fact is that Israel, God's own people, has not sought God's righteousness but its own (9. 30–10. 3). Here we have to make our choice between mutually exclusive alternatives. Moses says: 'Do the righteousness of the law and you shall live.' But Christ is the end of the law unto righteousness to all who believe. There is only one way to life: confess Jesus as Lord and believe heartily in His resurrection. Now belief presupposes hearing and hearing presupposes preaching and preaching presupposes sending. God did send the Word to Israel: but Israel would not believe (4–21). Does this mean that God has cast off Israel? No, He has seen to it that there is always a remnant—but it is a remnant 'according to the election of grace'—chosen by Him on the basis of pure kindness. It thus upsets the principle upon which Israel was trying to build (11. 1–6). But the rest God hardened (7–10). But did God purpose their destruction? No— He purposed the salvation of the Gentiles—and of Jews as well, by grace (11–12). So it comes to this. The one olive tree which God planted is all holy. But natural branches were broken off, and wild slips were grafted in, contrary to nature. On what principle? That of faith. They were cut off because of unbelief: you have your status in Israel only by faith. There is no room for glorying in high-mindedness. God, who cut off the natural branches, can well cut off the grafts. Therefore fear God. God, who grafted in wild slips, is perfectly capable of re-grafting the natural branches (13–24). And that is, in fact, His purpose. God's gifts and calling are irrevocable. He does not go back on them. But His salvation is all of mercy, and mercy absolutely excludes self-righteousness. Therefore 'he has shut up all into disobedience that he may have mercy upon all'. How great and unsearchable is His wisdom! (25–35).

No one can deny, I think, that the crucial word in this whole argument is the word 'faith'. The text on which the whole is founded is 'the just shall live by faith'. And in the light of the actual argument we can well accept Bishop Nygren's re-translation and say 'He who by faith is righteous shall live.' The blessing of eternal life belongs to those who have faith-righteousness. We are justified by faith; Christ's work is a propitiation by faith; Abraham was justified by faith, and it is by faith only that we can be reckoned as Abraham's seed: by faith we are saved; by unbelief the Jews were cut off from God's covenant and by faith Gentiles have their standing in it. One can almost say that at every key point in the argument the essential word is faith—almost, but not quite, because at one key point the whole argument appears to rest on baptism. But of that we shall speak later. Here it is sufficient to draw attention to the overwhelming weight of argument in favour of the statement that faith is, from the human side, the constitutive fact of membership in the people of God. One can practically sum up the whole argument in the Johannine statement that to believe is to have 'life in His name'.

This stress upon faith is deliberately directed against a counter-stress upon the 'works of the law'. As in Galatians, two spheres or principles of existence are portrayed as absolutely mutually exclusive. In one salvation is hoped for by obedience to the law, but in fact sin is in control, law becomes a tool in sin's hands and the result is bondage and death. In the other salvation is given as a gift of sheer grace, and received in faith, and here the Holy Spirit rules and the issue is freedom and life. And again—as in Galatians—the apostle argues that this has been from the beginning God's way of salvation, that Abraham was justified by faith, and that the law is given not to deliver us, but to show up sin in its true character and so to drive us to grace.

But there is another factor in the argument, a question which was not so explicitly dealt with in the Epistle to the Galatians, but to which in this Epistle St. Paul returns again and again. It is the question of God's faithfulness to His covenant with Israel. In Galatians he is dealing with the straightforward issue—law or grace. Here the treatment of that issue is involved with the question of the place in God's redemptive plan of the visible community of Israel. It is this that gives the argument much of its complexity. For the two questions can neither be identified nor separated.

God justifies men by free grace, and man's part is to believe. That is for the apostle a clear and unassailable certainty. But how does He do it? It is not done by some private and secret transaction between God and each individual soul, but publicly—as it were—upon the plane of history. He made a covenant with Abraham 'and his seed'. He called Israel as a people to be His people, to be His holy nation, His royal priesthood. He has established a visible congregation with visible signs. It is emphatically to this congregation—to the actual historic community of Israel—that He has given 'the adoption, the glory, the covenants, the law, the service of God and the promises', and it is to this community that Christ in His human nature belongs. 'Salvation', as the Lord Himself said, 'is from the Jews'.

But that quotation reminds one of the verse which immediately follows it: 'Salvation is from the Jews. But the hour cometh, and now is, when the true worshippers shall worship the Father in spirit and truth.' A new hour has struck. Out of the womb of the old Israel, the new Israel—Israel after the Spirit—is born. Not that it is wholly new: it is, as St. Paul says, 'witnessed to by the law and the prophets'. What is now revealed, he says, is a righteousness of God through faith in Jesus Christ unto all them that believe, without distinction. And in this new dispensation all glorying, he says, is excluded. *There is now no possibility for anyone to claim that he belongs to God's people by right.* No man has rights before God. Righteousness is by faith, by complete dependence on the gracious promises of God. There is no other.

The Jews had thus misunderstood their position in relation to God and to the Gentile world. They had not understood what the righteousness of God is. From the true premise that God had entered into a covenant with Abraham and his seed, they drew the false conclusion that, if they kept their side of the covenant, they had a status before God as of right, from which Gentiles were excluded. With a zeal which the apostle recognised but could not praise, they sought with more and more elaborate detail to fulfil their side of the covenant, to obey every precept of the divine law, and so to merit the status of sonship. The apostle describes this by saying that they had not submitted themselves to the righteousness of God but had gone about to establish their own. For God's righteousness, the righteousness which alone is counted as righteousness in His sight, is simply that which casts itself in loving trust and gratitude upon His grace: it is the very antithesis of that so-called righteousness which a man seeks to have when he tries to merit God's favour by his own good works. God did indeed enter into a covenant with Abraham and his seed, but the Jews misunderstood both the nature of the covenant and the manner of its inheritance. In the first place what was the relationship between God and Abraham on which the covenant was founded? It was a relationship of pure grace on God's side and pure trust on Abraham's. It was that relationship which was signified and sealed by circumcision. In the second place, succession to the covenant was not by merely natural descent from Abraham and not even by observance of the sign of circumcision: if it had been so, the original terms of the covenant would have been violated by the manner of its succession, for men could have been able to claim merely by the fact of their physical descent from Abraham and their observance of the outward signs of the covenant that they belonged to the covenant people. No, the inheritance is 'according to promise'. It depends, as the original covenant did, upon the free grace of God on one side and men's response of trust on the other.

Under the former dispensation it was possible for this to be misunderstood. But now the true nature of God's righteousness has been manifested in such a way that the whole meaning of God's dealing with His people is revealed, and that all reliance on any supposed human status is absolutely excluded. In the presence of the Cross no one, Jew or Gentile, can claim rights before God. All alike have sinned, and all alike are offered free justification by faith. And God has sealed this relationship between Himself and His people by a new seal—the gift of the Holy Spirit—the spirit by whom Jesus Himself was anointed. The presence of that seal makes it unthinkable that we should add to it the old seal of circumcision. To do so would imply an attempt to re-establish human claims upon God's grace: it would be to seek to make a fair show in the flesh. The new covenant has indeed its visible signs—the baptism which Jesus Himself underwent and which was the occasion of the anointing by the Spirit, and the supper which He Himself instituted as the effective sign of the new covenant in His blood. A visible community is the counterpart of the covenant. But the substance of the covenant itself is always grace and faith.

It is in the light of these facts that we are to understand the seeming complexity of God's dealings with Israel. To use a trite metaphor, His tactics must vary but His fundamental strategy is the same. He may lay Himself open to charges of inconsistency and infidelity to His promises, but a deeper understanding of His promises will show that all that He has done has sprung from one unchanging purpose—to have mercy upon all. But mercy must find ways of breaking down that which resists mercy— namely, self-righteousness. When Israel, which had been called into a covenant of pure grace, made that covenant a ground for claiming human rights against God, God gave them over to the hardening of heart which is self-righteousness. But, because His gifts and His calling are irrevocable, He kept a remnant—chosen again by His pure grace, and not at all upon a basis of merit—to be the true witnesses to the covenant of grace. And—as He had forewarned through the prophets—He called the Gentiles, those who were 'No people', to take the place of the unbelieving Jews. On what basis? Again on the basis of pure grace and—from the human side—faith alone. That is the only standing-ground that any human being has in the people of God. Jews were cut off for their unbelief; Gentiles have their standing by faith. And God's purpose is that thereby unbelieving Jews shall be brought to faith and so obtain mercy again. Not only at the establishment of the covenant but at every moment of it, we have to deal with the living God who offers to man His free, boundless, sovereign, and undeservable grace, and who asks from, and gives to, those who will receive it the one thing acceptable to God—the faith that hopes only in God, and works through a love which is the overflow of the love wherewith God first loved us. It is by faith alone that we have access to this grace wherein we stand.

II

This central and essential strand of biblical teaching must be held firmly in our hands throughout all our search for the answer to our initial question: 'What is the manner of our incorporation in Christ?' But it leads us immediately to a new question. It is by faith that we are given our standing-ground before God—faith in God. But how is God presented to our faith? In Jesus Christ. There is one mediator, given once for all, at the centre of world history, by whom we are reconciled to God. How then is Jesus Christ presented to our faith who live nineteen centuries after His incarnation? In what way is He made contemporary with us, so that we may believe in Him? To His contemporaries in Galilee and Judaea in the days of His flesh He was present to the sight and hearing and touch of men and they were invited to put their trust in Him and be made whole. But how is He present to us today?

Orthodox Protestants have unhesitatingly answered, 'He is present in the word and sacraments of the Gospel.' In the word of the Gospel truly read and preached, and in the sacraments which He gave, duly administered, Christ Himself is present in His saving power, to evoke faith, to reconcile sinful man with holy God, to build up the Church which is His body by drawing all men to Himself. 'Wherever', says Luther, 'you see this Word preached, believed, confessed and acted on, there do not doubt that there must be a true *ecclesia sancta catholica* . . . for God's word does not go away empty.'[1] Similarly, he says, the catholic Church is known by the presence of the sacraments of baptism and of the altar rightly administered, taught, believed and used according to Christ's ordinance. It does not matter who preaches and who gives the sacraments, nor do they require the authority of the Pope, for the word and sacraments are God's, not men's. By them God does His own work. Similarly Calvin writes: 'Wherever we see the word of God sincerely preached and heard, wherever we see the sacraments administered according to the institution of Christ, there we cannot have any doubt that the Church of God has some existence, since his promise cannot fail, "Where two or three are gathered together in my name, there am I in the midst of them"' (Inst. IV, 1, 9).

[1] On the Council and the Churches. Holman Ed., V, p. 271.

D

No one, I think, would seriously wish to deny what these statements affirm. But it is a different matter when we go on to consider whether these statements convey the whole truth, and whether there is no place for other and distinct considerations in answering the question, 'How is Christ present to us today?' The Reformers have given us an intensely dynamic conception of the Church. They took with immense seriousness the truth that the Church is the body of Christ, that He is ever dynamically creative in it and through it, that He, the living Lord, is in very truth present today in His Church through the word and sacraments with power to create and re-create, to convert, to reconcile, to root up and pull down, to build and to plant. The obvious defect of this conception, as it has manifested itself in the subsequent centuries of Protestant development, is that it gives no real place to the continuing life of the Church as one fellowship binding the generations together in Christ. It makes of the Church practically a series of totally disconnected events in which, at each moment and place at which the word and sacraments of the Gospel are set forth, the Church is there and then called into being by God's creative power. I am aware that I am exaggerating in order to make the point clear; nevertheless it is difficult not to feel, in reading, for instance, Karl Barth's paper in the Amsterdam Volume on the Church, that this dynamic doctrine of the Church is taken to almost this extreme point. He introduces all his key paragraphs with the phrase, 'The congregation (*ecclesia*) is an event (*Ereignis*).' The immediate relation of the Church in every moment of its being to its living Lord could not be more powerfully expressed. But there seems to be no place in the picture for a continuing historical institution, nor for any organic relation between congregations in different places and times. In so far as the Church possesses the character of a continuing and widely spread historical institution it seems, on this view, to have fallen away from its proper centre. The eschatological has completely pushed out the historical.

We may indicate the element which is lacking in this view by starting from either of two ends—from the incarnate Christ Himself, or from the Church as it actually meets us today. Taking the latter first, we must ask: Does not this Protestant view err in isolating the word and the sacraments from their actual context in the on-going life of the Church? The word and sacraments are never isolated events. They are never—if one may speak crudely—let down from heaven at the end of a string. We may agree that they are creative in relation to the Church, but they do not create the Church *de novo*, or *ex nihilo*. Every setting forth of the word and sacraments of the Gospel is an event in the life of an actually existing Christian Church or fellowship of some kind, presupposes such a fellowship, and cannot be severed from it. We shall not question that they are the word and sacraments of Christ. But also we cannot close our eyes to the fact that, in their actual transmission and administration, and in the congregational life which forms their inevitable context, they are the words and acts of that particular Christian body. This is true whether the one who speaks or administers is speaking in the midst of established Christendom, or as the very first ambassador of Christ to a completely pagan culture. That the life of the Church in which he is nourished will profoundly affect the manner of his setting forth of the word is obvious. But this does not exhaust the point. In the written scriptures, and still more in the sacraments, there is a hard core of resistance to the changes and chances, the distortions and vagaries of on-going Christian history. But even these things do not come—so to say—naked. They come clothed in the forms of the Church, and the forms of the Church's life will provide the most influential commentary on them. The world will always, consciously or unconsciously, judge what the Church says by what it is. They will interpret the printed epistle by the living epistle.

And this leads us to look at the same point from the other end, from the angle of the New Testament. It is true that Christ gave to His disciples His word and sacraments. But He did not give them naked. He left no written code which should keep inviolate for all time the essential message, and the essential requirements for the due observance of His sacraments. A vast amount of scholarly labour has been spent in trying to discover precisely that thing which the Lord Himself did not choose to provide. What He left behind was a fellowship, and He entrusted to it the task of being His representative to the world. 'As the Father hath sent me,' He said, 'even so send I you.' They were to be His representatives, His plenipotentiaries. He endowed them with His own spirit to be His witnesses. They were given His authority to cast out sickness and evil. To receive them was to receive Him, and to reject them was to reject Him. We are not here considering how far these words refer to the apostles alone and how far to the whole body. The point is that if we ask, what was the explicit provision which Jesus made for the extension of His saving power to the whole world, we must answer that it was the fellowship which He called, trained, endowed, and sent forth. And if, in the light of that unquestionable fact, we go on to ask again our fundamental question—how is Jesus present to us today?—it is surely clear that at least a very central part of the answer must be: He is present in His people, His apostolic fellowship. It is surely significant that, while believers are spoken of as those who are 'begotten of God', Paul can write to his converts in Corinth: 'In Christ Jesus I begat you through the gospel.'

It will be our task in the next lecture to examine more thoroughly the implications of this answer, and the distortions which have arisen through taking it in isolation as the clue to the Church's nature. But before turning to this, it is important to say something about the practical out-working in Protestant history of the theological defect which, as we are suggesting, was present at the source.

1. Firstly, it has led to an over-intellectualising of the content of the word 'faith'. This is an inevitable consequence of the initial theoretical setting of word and sacraments in isolation over against the continuing life of the fellowship. If we begin by saying that the Church exists where the word is truly preached and the sacraments rightly administered, we are immediately involved in the attempt to answer the question, 'What is correct doctrine and correct administration?' In fact, the latter question has tended to drop out of the centre of Protestant discussion, for the word was really central and the sacrament was conceived essentially as the word made visible. 'The Word,' says Luther, 'is the one perpetual and infallible mark of the Church.' The natural result of this position is that the question of doctrinal correctness becomes the all-important one. And, *ex hypothesi*, this question has to be discussed in isolation, apart from consideration of the character of the fellowship in which the doctrine is taught. The Church is defined in terms of agreement about doctrine, and this doctrinal agreement must be agreement on paper. A written theological statement becomes the one determinative centre of the Church's life.

In saying this I must immediately add that I realise how much more can and should be said in its proper place. True doctrine will always be vital to the Church's life; there are plenty of examples outside of Protestantism of the treatment of Christian doctrine as a subject for intellectual jousting in a spirit far different from that Spirit whom Christ gave to His people. And of course the great reformers had the most vivid appreciation of the fact that we are united to Christ by something infinitely more than correctly formulated doctrine. Nevertheless when all this is fully acknowledged, as it must be, I think it is true that if we answer the question: 'How are we made incorporate in Christ?', *solely* in the words 'by hearing and believing the Gospel', and apart from the context of a continuing fellowship through which the Gospel comes to us, we become inevitably involved in an over-intellectualised conception of faith. Doctrinal agreement, which means agreement that can be formulated in written doctrinal statements, comes to be more and more regarded as the one essential basis for Christian unity. And the life of the Church comes to be centred in the teaching and acceptance of correct doctrine.

But of course the unity of believers with Christ and with one another in Him is of a far deeper nature than intellectual agreement. It is not in its essential nature an intellectual agreement at all, though necessarily it involves a certain amount of intellectual agreement about truths which can be expressed in propositional form. In its essential nature it is a work of the Holy Spirit binding us to one another in the love wherewith Christ loved us; and its essential human condition is the faith which consists in casting oneself wholly upon that love, and opening heart and mind and soul to its influence. Within that unity a vast amount of intellectual disagreement is possible, though such disagreement will never be other than painful. It is never to be acquiesced in, and believers must always be seeking to convince one another of the truth as they see it, and to learn from one another. But it can be borne when the Holy Spirit binds believers one to another in love, and it is made bearable by the assurance that one day we shall know as we have been known. The true character of this union of believers with one another in Christ is disastrously distorted when it is conceived of essentially in terms of doctrinal agreement. The effect of such distortion is to break the Christian fellowship up into rival parties, each based upon some one-sided doctrinal formulation, and eventually into completely separated bodies. The sad story is too well-known to require re-telling. I think it behoves us who are grateful heirs of the Reformation to consider penitently whether the tragic fragmentation of Christendom which followed the Reformation was not in part due to a theological defect at this point.

2. This leads immediately to the second distortion which—I suggest—springs from a defect in the reformers' doctrine of the Church. I refer to the virtual disappearance of the idea of the Church as a visible unity. Again, of course, one must immediately remind oneself that there are magnificent passages in the works of the great reformers describing the Church as the mother of us all, the sphere of forgiveness, the home outside of which is no salvation. But I submit that in the context of the ecumenical conversation of today, it is not enough for Protestant theologians to go on contentedly pointing to these passages. It is necessary to seek penitently and realistically for the source of the tendency to endless fissiparation which has characterised Protestantism in its actual history. How has it come about that the vast majority of Protestant Christians are content to see the Church of Jesus Christ split up into hundreds of separate sects, feel no sense of shame about such a situation, and sometimes even glory in it and claim the support of the New Testament for it? Where is the theological root of the error which can produce such an astounding blinding of the eyes of good Christian men and women? I submit that we are not responsible participants in the ecumenical conversation if we do not try to answer these questions.

Luther had to face the entire spiritual and political power of the Roman Church, to overthrow the theology which identified incorporation in Christ with submission to that power, and to assert the truth that the Church is ever being re-created by the living Christ present in His word and sacraments. In this titanic struggle it was inevitable that many violent and one-sided statements should have been made, and it is easy to find in his writings sentences which completely contradict the New Testament teaching about one Body and one Spirit, and leave no room at all for the unity of the Church as a visible community. 'How is it possible,' he asks, 'and whose reason can grasp it, that spiritual unity and material unity should be one and the same?' And a little later, 'All those who make the Christian Communion a material and outward thing, like other communities, are really Jews.' He draws an absolute distinction between what he calls 'the two churches', the 'natural essential real true inner Christendom and a man-made, external bodily Christendom',[1] though he allows that they ought not to be put asunder and that the latter always has some true Christians in it. This distinction has an extremely practical outcome in his doctrine regarding the ban.[2] He teaches that the Church's excommunication can only touch a man's relation with the external Christendom but cannot take away his inner communion with Christ, and that it is not the Church which delivers a man to Satan, but the sinner who delivers himself by his own sin and unbelief. This teaching obviously provided the basis upon which Luther and those who followed him could defy the papal ban, and it has similarly provided the basis upon which lesser men with less reason have gained the assurance that enabled them to separate from the visible communion of the Church in which they had been begotten and nurtured as Christians. Yet very plainly it is different from the teaching of the New Testament on the same subject. When Paul writes to the Corinthians[3] about the excommunication of the erring brother, it is very clear that he does *not* say or imply that it is simply a matter of the sinner cutting himself off. He calls for a very solemn and deliberate act of the fellowship—an act in which he himself is completely associated. Moreover this act is not regarded as merely a severance of external membership while leaving the man's spiritual relationship with Christ untouched. It is a matter of the most awful spiritual meaning—nothing less than delivering him to Satan. Surely we have to face the fact that, whatever we may make of it, Paul and his converts were alike working with a conception of the Church which made membership in it a tremendous spiritual reality. To be in its fellowship was to be in Christ, and to be cast out of it was to be delivered over to Satan. I find it quite impossible to reconcile the language of this passage with the language of Luther's sermon on the ban. This passage seems completely to exclude a conception of church membership as a merely external thing which can be severed without ultimate spiritual harm, distinguished from membership

---

[1] *The Papacy at Rome*, Luther. Holman Ed., I, p. 350, 352 and 355.
[2] Holman Ed., II, pp. 37-54.   [3] I Cor. 5. 9-13.

in Christ as a private matter over which the believer alone has final control. The passage, like the rest of the New Testament, surely assumes that there is a real people of God in the world, a real spiritual society, a real body of Christ actually present in the world, a place where the light of God really shines and the life of God really pulses, and that it makes the most awful and ultimate difference conceivable whether you are inside or outside of that place.

How far are we dealing here with extremes of expression forced out of Luther in the terrible pressure of events, and how far with a fundamental defect in doctrine? Certainly Luther was in that sermon fighting for the truth of the Gospel against error, and it was vital for the free course of the Gospel that he should not submit to the Church of Rome. But the doctrinal weapons which he forged for the battle against Rome are not in themselves sufficient as a total statement of the Church's nature. The ultimate problem of the Church, the seat of the perplexity which surrounds all systematic thought about it, is the fact that it is at once holy and sinful. No one since St. Paul has done more to make that clear than Luther. Most writing about the Church still fails primarily by failing to grasp the truth that Luther enunciated when he said that justification by faith is the article by which the Church stands or falls. Yet by substituting at this critical point for the true and biblical dialectic of holy and sinful, a false and unbiblical dialectic of outward and inward, visible and invisible, Luther himself helped profoundly to confuse the issue of the Reformation. By saying this I do not mean that it was possible for him to have acted otherwise. I have not the historical knowledge to make such a judgment, and in any case it would be impertinent to do so. I only mean that the actual effect of this teaching as it has shown itself in the subsequent history of Protestantism has been deeply harmful to the Church, because it has largely destroyed the conception of the Church's visible unity. It seems to me only honest to admit this.

The world apart from Christ knows enough of ideas of God round which men may group themselves according to their convictions, ideas which may more or less fully reflect the reality of the divine being. What God has given to the world in Christ is something different, an actual divine humanity, a real presence of God in human history, not a new idea about God, but God made man, and calling men into fellowship with Himself. And having taken humanity upon Himself He has not again divested Himself of it. As Son of Man He is at the right hand of the Father and His Spirit is given to the Church which is His body on earth. In Him, heaven and earth are truly joined. He sends His apostles forth to be His representatives and He promises His presence with them always. They are the beginnings of a real continuation of His redeeming work, an extension of the divine humanity— though in a different mode—through history, until its consummation at His coming again. This divine-human fellowship is a real visible community having its place in world history, even though the secret of its life is invisible and lies beyond world history. Christ has promised to be with it to the end of the world, and it is His presence which constitutes it. As against a view which found the constitutive fact of the Church in mere institutional continuity with the Church of the apostles, Luther was certainly right in asserting that it is the saving presence of the Living Christ which constitutes the Church, and that this saving activity of the Living Christ takes place in the preaching of the word and the giving of the sacraments. But when the Church is defined *simply* as that which is continually (or perhaps one really should say repeatedly) created from above by the work of Christ in the word and sacraments, then a real distortion has taken place. The relation between the word and sacraments on the one hand and the Church on the other is not *simply* that the latter is the creation of the former. The word is preached and the sacraments are administered in and by the Church as well as to the Church, and Christ, the Head of the body, acts in them, both through and for the Church. It is extremely difficult to state in words the profound mystery of the relation between Christ and the Church, but it is certain that it cannot be done by picturing the word and sacraments simply as instruments of Christ's saving power standing over against the Church, and the Church simply as that which is created by them.

It is a natural consequence of this over-simplification that the visible unity of the Church comes to be regarded as a matter of minor importance, since the continuing fellowship is no longer seen as the bearer of God's saving purpose. 'The essence, life and nature of the Church,' says Luther, 'is not a bodily assembly but an assembly of hearts in one faith.' And again, 'A spiritual unity

... is of itself sufficient to make a Church.'[1] This language is
uncomfortably unlike that of the Bible with its stress upon an
actual visible fellowship. The difficulty about what is purely
spiritual is that it is apt to become purely private. We are not
discarnate spirits and we enter into spiritual communion one with
another only through our sense experience of sight, sound and
touch. Without this we quickly become prisoners of our own
self-hood. The one body spoken of in the New Testament is not
the contrary of the one Spirit, but its implicate. To place them
in ultimate opposition to one another is fatal to a true doctrine
of the Church. Yet one cannot help admitting that over and over
again this is precisely what Luther did.

In his very clear and persuasive statement of the Lutheran
doctrine of the Church in the Lund volume, Professor Schlink
tries to meet the difficulty while taking his stand firmly on the
classical Lutheran ground.[2] He says: 'The Church is constituted
by the event (*Ereignis*) of the preaching of the Gospel and the
administering of the sacraments, and so by Christ Himself acting
through and present in Gospel and sacraments', and, elsewhere,
'The Congregation of believers cannot exist at all without Gospel
and sacraments. Without preaching and sacraments it would
dissolve into nothing and would never have arisen.' He claims
that by this 'the idea of the Church is separated from a false
ontology and also from dissolution into a succession of individual
acts without any continuity. The continuity of the Church consists in the identity of the Gospel preached ever anew, and it
thereby becomes visible.' But this is to say that the Church is
not a continuing society in the ordinary sense at all. Identity of
doctrine is one thing: continuity of a social organism is another.
The issue comes to a point in his reference to Article XIV of the
Augsburg Confession which lays down that no one ought in the
Church to teach publicly or administer the sacraments unless duly
called (*nisi rite vocatus*). This phrase is surely a necessary expression
of the truth which all ecclesiastical bodies accept in practice,
whatever their theory of the matter, that the Church has a certain
authority over the preaching of the word and the administration
of the sacraments. This becomes clear when she authorises a
minister to perform these functions. Yet this obviously means
that the Church is not *merely* an event continually created by the

[1] Holman Ed., I, p. 349.   [2] *The Nature of the Church*, pp. 54–70.

word and sacraments. The question, 'Who is authorised to give or withold authority to minister the word and sacraments?' has to be answered, and this involves the whole question of the orderly transmission of authority from generation to generation within the Church, and therefore its continuity as one visible society. The crux of the matter is, of course, the interpretation of the word 'duly' (*rite*). Professor Schlink says that the phrase '*nisi rite vocatus*' means 'without a call to the office founded by Christ', and insists that succession in ministerial office rests not upon a succession of ordinations but rather on the identity of the Gospel and sacraments which Christ instituted. But this still does not enable us to escape the problem involved in the word 'duly', or the question, 'How may we know that a person is in fact called to this office?' In fact, the living Church must decide. Nobody can escape the actual responsibility of living in the flesh and in history. By setting the continuity of true doctrine over against the continuity of a historical organism, Protestantism has not escaped from the conditions that govern all human social existence. It is a matter of common observation that new Christian sects have an irresistible tendency to develop more and more of the characteristics of the so-called historic Churches, and, in particular, to develop a very high regard for their own continued historical existence as particular societies. But what Protestantism has done is to weaken very seriously the sense of the unity and continuity of the Church as one people of God in all ages and all places, continually drawing all men out of the narrowness and poverty of their private spiritual experiences and setting them in a great fellowship which, as it has conceived them and brought them to the new birth, will also nourish and sustain them to the end, enfolding them in the arms of a charity as wide as the arms of the Cross. And while we will certainly agree that this result was not intended by the Reformers, I think we must admit that it is not the result of accidental or extraneous causes but goes back to a defect in their fundamental doctrine of the Church. The Church cannot be defined *simply* as that which is constituted by the event of the preaching of the Gospel and the administering of the sacraments. It belongs to its true nature that it is a continuing historical society, that society which was constituted and sent forth once for all by Jesus Christ.

III

THE BODY OF CHRIST

In the previous lecture we looked briefly at the teaching of the New Testament and especially of St. Paul, that the relationship which we have with God through Christ is constituted from God's side by pure, free grace, and from man's by faith. We tried to weigh the arguments by which the apostles Peter and Paul met the demands of those who desired to add to faith circumcision. We reminded ourselves that the great apostolic affirmations about faith—that the righteousness we have in Christ is by faith alone, that the life of the man in Christ is by faith alone—belong to the very central citadel of Gospel truth which can never be surrendered. We then went on to ask how Christ is made present for our believing today and considered the characteristically Protestant answer, that He is present in the true preaching of the word and the right administration of the sacraments. We saw reason to think that this answer—true in what it affirms—has to be criticised for failing to give place, in its statement of the manner of Christ's presence for faith, to the continuing life of the Christian fellowship. We now turn, therefore, to look at the type of answer to our main question which concentrates upon precisely this element, which affirms that we are made incorporate in Christ primarily and essentially by sacramental incorporation into the life of His Church.

I

One of the difficulties of trying to set forth the biblical basis for this view is the fact that, in the Bible, it is simply assumed rather than deliberately argued. Instead of examining a deliberate argument upon a particular issue, therefore, one must try to attend to what lies behind arguments and narratives as their constant presupposition. Without attempting any very logical arrangement with precise definitions, let me try to indicate something of the biblical evidence in the matter.

1. We may begin with the fact, to which frequent reference has been made, that at the heart and centre of the earthly ministry of the incarnate Christ was the choosing, training and sending forth of a band of apostles.[1] If His purpose had been to provide for all succeeding generations of mankind a revelation of God which could be embodied in a series of verbal statements of absolute inerrancy, or an infallible code of conduct, He could have left a written deposit as Mahomet is said to have done. A great deal of subsequent thinking seems to assume that this is what He ought to have done. But it is precisely what He did not do. He chose twelve men that they might be with Him and that He might send them forth. Being with Him they received, not so much a formal course of instruction in divine truth as an introduction into the intimacy of His Spirit. At the very end He told them that He had much more yet to tell them. If divine revelation means a complete communication of the whole counsel of God to men, then we have it on His own authority that He did not give it. What He did was to reveal *Himself* to them and in so doing to reveal the Father. By living with Jesus in the flesh, seeing, hearing, touching Him in whom the Spirit dwelt fully, they are prepared to be themselves the dwelling-place of the same Spirit (John 14. 17), to share the risen life of Christ (v. 19), to know who He is (v. 20), and to learn all things (v. 26 and 16. 13). And in sending them forth to teach and to have authority over the powers of evil, He gave them His own commission to represent His Person in the fullest sense. As He represents the Father, they are to represent Him to the world. 'As the Father hath sent me, even so send I you'. 'He who receives you receives me, and he who receives me receives Him who sent me.' And because they are His apostles, they have His authority in the spiritual world. They have the authority to command disease and all the powers of evil, as He had, and in the Acts we see them unhesitatingly exercising this authority. This sense of the unity, one may almost say identity, of Jesus and His apostles, and indeed all who believe on Him through this word, is expressed with great fullness in the prayer of our Lord on the night of His passion. Here the Lord says that He has given to them the glory which He had with the Father, in order that they may be one in

[1] On this section see *The Unity of the Church in the New Testament*, Stig Hanson (Uppsala).

the same unity with which the Father and the Son are one, and that by this perfect unity the world may know that the Father has sent Him. It is congruous with this thought of the identity of Christ and His people that the same authority to forgive sins which in Him was so scandalous to the Jewish leaders should be bestowed upon the Church also. 'Whose soever sins ye remit, they are remitted unto them; and whose soever sins ye retain, they are retained.' There can be no question, in the light of such evidence as this, that Jesus intended to be represented in all the plenitude of His power, by His own chosen and commissioned people.

2. In the second place, this element in the Gospel record is wholly congruous with the biblical revelation as a whole, in which God's saving purpose is executed through the calling of a particular people, one tribe among all the tribes of the earth. The thread which binds the whole Bible story together is emphatically not the history of an idea but the history of a people. Let me put this sharply by saying that, in the Bible, the people of God is at no time conceived of as a voluntary association of those who have agreed with one another in accepting and carrying out certain convictions about God. It is conceived of as something which has been constituted by the mighty act of God, an act springing from His pure grace, and preceding the first dawnings of man's understanding of it and acceptance of its implications. While Israel is a slave people, sunk in degrading bondage and without faith or hope, God stretches forth His hand to redeem them, to take them out of the prison-house, and to set them in the land which He has chosen for them. At Mount Sinai they are brought face to face with Him who has done this, and invited to understand and accept its meaning: 'Ye have seen what I did unto the Egyptians, and how I bare you on eagles' wings, and brought you unto myself. Now therefore, if ye will obey my voice indeed, and keep my covenant, then ye shall be a peculiar treasure unto me from among all peoples: for all the earth is mine: and ye shall be unto me a kingdom of priests, and an holy nation' (Ex. 19. 4-6). And all the people answered together and said: 'All that the Lord hath spoken we will do.' Faith and obedience are required of them, yet these are wholly subsequent to and answering to what has already been done. They do not constitute the people, and it is indeed very clear from the narrative that the

people so far from being faithful and obedient were a stiff-necked and unbelieving nation. God's way of salvation is not by enabling a number of individuals to grasp the truth—either by mystical union, or by intellectual enquiry, or by being given one universal and inerrant revelation in code or book; it is by calling a people to Himself, that they may be with Him and that He may send them forth. When the prophets denounce idolatry, injustice and vice in Israel, it is because Israel *is* the people of God, and is bound by the covenant which He has established by His mighty acts. In the epistles Christians are addressed as this people of God. They are His royal priesthood, His holy nation. The Gentiles who have believed are described as slips grafted into the one olive tree which is Israel, and which exists before their faith, and will continue to exist even if, by their unbelief, they have to be cut off. What is true of the Gospel story is true of the whole Bible: it is the story of a people which is central.

3. It is also relevant here to point to the general teaching of the Bible about the solidarity of the individual in the group, for in this also the New Testament is based upon the Old. It is of course true, and profoundly important, that the Old Testament records a developing understanding of the ultimate and unsharable responsibility of the individual before God, and that in the teaching of Jesus we find unsurpassable expressions of the unique preciousness of every single individual to God. Yet—because of the basic biblical teaching about the creation of all things by God—this never passes over into a denial of the solidarities in which the individual is set. On the basis of the faith that God is creator of all things, of things visible no less than of things invisible, and that He has made man a body-soul unity, and that He has made him male and female that the twain should be one flesh, it is impossible to retreat into a view which leaves man ultimately alone with God and relegates to some sort of lower level of significance all the natural, psychological, economic, and biological solidarities in which his life is lived. To attempt to state truly the relation between these two aspects of human existence is of course a vast and difficult matter into which I shall not venture to enter. But it is surely clear that, on the basis of the biblical teaching, while we are precluded from treating the individual merely as a product of the various solidarities in which he is set, we are likewise precluded from treating these solidarities merely as the products

of a multitude of individual decisions. The importance of this point is very obvious when we come to deal with the teaching of St. Paul about the body, to which we turn in a moment. It is also significant in this connection that in the Gospels and Acts, while faith is in general required of those upon whom Christ performs His mighty works of healing, it is clear that the faith of family and friends, the faith of a group, may be as important as or more important than that of the individual. The paralytic man was healed when Jesus saw the faith of his four friends, the centurion's servant in response to the believing prayer of his master, and the Syro-Phoenician girl in response to that of her mother. At Philippi Paul tells the jailor, 'Believe on the Lord Jesus and thou shalt be saved—thou and thy house,' and that very night the whole household is forthwith baptised. St. Paul's teaching that the unbelieving partner in a marriage with a believer is sanctified in the other, and that the children also are sanctified, is congruous with this whole biblical attitude. It is taken for granted that God deals with men not only as individuals in the solitude of personal responsibility but also in their natural solidarities of family, household and nation.

4. This leads us to note a further characteristic of the biblical thinking which forms the context of the doctrine of the Church. In the Bible salvation is concerned with the whole created order. The whole visible world is ascribed to God, and it is, in its essential nature, good. Though the fall of man has mysteriously corrupted nature also, yet nature itself is not evil. Nor is it merely the neutral setting of man's spiritual life. It has its own part to play in glorifying God. And its renewal is part of the consummation for which at present the whole creation groans and travails in longing. In particular man's physical frame is not treated as the merely temporary envelope of an immortal spirit. Man is treated as a living whole, and his eternal future is conceived of in terms of the resurrection of the body rather than of the immortality of the soul. The final consummation of all things is conceived to include the renewal of the whole created universe, and of man's body, and the restoration of its lost harmony in the joy of God's service.

These elements in the biblical teaching are familiar and I allude to them only to point out that what is true of the doctrines of creation and of the last things will also govern the doctrine of the Church and of the means of grace. The Church, as the sphere wherein the first-fruits of the age to come are experienced within this present age, will not be a merely spiritual reality whose outward forms and signs will be a sort of dead husk enclosing the living seed. On the contrary, it is in accordance with the whole biblical standpoint that the sphere of salvation should be a visible fellowship marked by visible signs wherein God uses material means to convey His saving power, and wherein, therefore, there is an earnest and foretaste of the restoration of creation to its true harmony in and for God's glory, and of man to his true relation to the created world.

These statements raise, of course, vast issues concerning the nature of the Gospel sacraments, the solution of which will involve in turn our whole understanding of the relation of the mind of man to the world which he knows by his sense-experience. Into these issues I do not pretend now to be able to enter. The one thing that seems clear is that God has joined these two together, making man a body-soul unity, and that every attempt to separate them leads to disaster.[1] On the one hand the Bible is full of reminders that God looks upon the heart and judges the reins, that mere outward conformity to His commandments or performance of His worship is not enough. But on the other hand, every attempt to develop a purely spiritual religion emancipated entirely from outward forms must part company completely with the Bible. It is utterly characteristic of the Bible as a whole that when Jesus speaks to Nicodemus about the necessity for the new birth, He speaks not simply of being born of the Spirit but of being born of water and the Spirit. The stark materialism of that sentence is apt to offend very deeply our sense of what it means to be spiritual beings called into fellowship with God who is Spirit. But it seems to me to be completely congruous with the whole picture which the Bible gives us of man's nature and place in the world, that the entrance to that fellowship should be by the door of baptism in water, and that the Son of God Himself should enter into His earthly ministry through that same lowly door.

5. This leads us to a brief reminder of the place of the sacra-

[1] The modern developments of psycho-somatic medicine are of deep interest in this connection, for they appear to indicate a recovery of the biblical understanding of the human person as a unity.

E

ments in the constitution of the Church. The opening of the Gospel narrative is the story of the baptism of Jesus by John. He who is sent to baptise with the Holy Spirit is Himself first baptised in water, taking His place humbly in the crowd of penitent men and women who go out to John in the wilderness. And in this baptism He Himself receives the anointing of the Spirit and the assurance of sonship. In this act baptism is itself transformed, for Jesus in His baptism took upon Himself the Cross of the Suffering Servant, and His baptism in Jordan was thus a sort of prolepsis of the baptism which He was to accomplish on Calvary, a baptism for the whole world. But in being transformed baptism was not abolished. On the contrary the very first preaching of the Gospel ends with the summons to 'Repent and be baptised,' and from the day of Pentecost onwards the whole preaching and practice of the apostolic Church is congruous with the commission which the risen Christ had given them: 'Go ye into all the world; make disciples of all nations; baptise; teach.' Throughout the New Testament admission into the new covenant with all its privileges and responsibilities is by faith and baptism. When *we* put those two words together we are immediately conscious of difficulties. How is faith related to baptism? If there is really faith, is baptism necessary? What is the use of baptism if there is no faith? Is baptism only a useful sign and seal? Or is it really true that God has circumscribed the blessings of the new covenant with this rite? So far as I can see, the New Testament writers are totally unconscious of these difficulties. It is simply taken for granted that baptism is that by which we were made members of the body of Christ and participants in the Spirit. St. Paul in the midst of his tremendous arguments in Galatians and Romans, when he is battling for the truth that faith alone justifies, can without the slightest awkwardness refer to baptism as that by which we were incorporated in Christ. To the Galatians he writes: 'Ye are all sons of God, through faith, in Jesus Christ. For as many of you as were baptised into Christ did put on Christ . . . ye all are one man in Christ Jesus' (Gal. 3. 26–28). To the Romans he answers the fundamental attack upon the whole doctrine of justification by faith, the accusation that it makes the moral struggle unnecessary, by reminding them of their baptism. 'Are you ignorant that all we who were baptised into Christ Jesus were baptised into his death? We were buried therefore with him through baptism into death: that like as Christ was raised from the dead through the glory of the Father, so we also might walk in newness of life' (Rom. 6. 3–4). To the Ephesians he can write of 'one baptism' as among the great central verities which the believer must keep ever in mind, along with 'one Lord, one faith . . . one God and Father of all' (Eph. 4. 5–6). The Colossians are reminded that they were buried with Christ in baptism, wherein they were also raised with Him through faith in the working of God, who raised Him from the dead (Col. 2. 12). In spite of everything that Paul has to say about faith as the ground of our justification, of our sonship, of our receiving of the Spirit, of our living 'in Christ', he also speaks, equally plainly and unambiguously, of baptism as that by which we are made members of Christ. The body of Christ in which Christians are members is a visible body, entrance into which is marked by the visible sign of baptism. In the same way the centre of its on-going life is the visible sign of bread broken together. As baptism marked Jesus' entry into His earthly ministry, so the institution of the supper marked the consummation of it. It was His last act in the midst of His disciples while with them in the flesh. The final conflict with the prince of this world was at hand. The faith of the disciples was crumbling. In a few short hours all under-standing and all obedience would be carried away in the flood of disaster. They would all forsake Him, and He would have to go forward utterly alone to make the final offering of obedience on behalf of all men, and win on behalf of all men the final battle. At that moment, when all faith was crumbling, He staked all upon a deed. He took bread and wine, told them, 'This is my body given for you, this is my blood shed for you. Do this in remembrance of me,' and then went out to suffer and die alone. And on the first Lord's Day, when the victory was won, but the disciples were defeated and broken, it was in the breaking of the bread that He was made known to them in His risen power. When all landmarks were submerged in the flood of disaster, and stories of His resurrection seemed but an idle tale, it was this utterly simple word, 'Do this', which rallied them, and gave them the place at which the meaning of what had happened could be made plain. And thereafter it was in this fellowship at the Lord's table, in breaking the bread and sharing the cup as He had commanded, that they were made actual participants in His body and blood, members incorporate in His risen life by participation in His dying.

6. This leads us naturally to consider the teaching of St. Paul on the Church as the Body of Christ.[1] We cannot here pretend to do justice to the immense mass of material on this subject, but can only call attention by way of reminder to a few points which bear upon our argument. For St. Paul the life of the Christian is life in Christ, and it can at the same time be described as the life of Christ in the believer. It is a participation in the life of Christ who is even now at the right hand of the Father. It is this because it is first a participation in His death. The Christian has died with Christ and his life is hid with Christ in God (Col. 3. 3). He is crucified with Christ and now Christ lives in him (Gal. 2. 20). He has put off the flesh-body in the circumcision of Christ (Col. 2. 11), put off the old man and put on the new which is being renewed unto knowledge after the image of Him that created him (Col. 3. 9–10). Christians were made dead to the law through the body of Christ, that they should be joined to another—to Him who was raised from the dead (Rom. 7. 4), and in the context it is made clear that the word 'joined' refers back to the metaphor of the union of man and wife in one flesh.

The crucial phrase in this last quotation is 'through the body of Christ'. It refers *both* to the death of Christ's body of flesh once for all on the Cross, *and* to the union of believers with Him in His risen body of which they have been made members. By being a member of Christ's body, the Christian has a share both in His putting off of the body of flesh wherein He gained the victory over all the powers of sin and death and law; and in His risen life —the life of a Spirit-filled body in which the Spirit quickens even the mortal bodies of the members.

If we are to understand the apostle's language we must, of course, come as close as possible to understanding what he meant by the word 'body'. The first thing which is quite clear is that, for him, the terms body and spirit are not contraries. More often they are correlates. The true, basic, and constantly repeated contradiction is between spirit and flesh. Body is a term which can

---

[1] In this section I am indebted to the brilliant study of St. Paul's teaching on the subject by J. A. T. Robinson, *The Body*, and to Cerfaux, *Le Christ dans Theologie de Saint Paul*.

be used in close connection with either of them. There is a body of the flesh and there is a spiritual body. The body of the flesh is that wherein Christ came at His incarnation and wrought our atonement on the Cross. The spiritual body (I Cor. 15. 44) is that in which He was raised from the dead and lives for ever, and not only so, but also that in which He gives life to those who believe on Him. (The last Adam became a life-giving Spirit—I Cor. 15. 45.) To say that Christ is our life, and to say that we are members in the body of Christ is—for Paul—to say the same thing. Consequently the two terms appear bracketed together as though the connection were simply a matter of course. 'There is one body and one Spirit, even as also ye were called in one hope of your calling' (Eph. 4. 4). 'In one Spirit were we all baptised into one body' (I Cor. 12. 13; see also Eph. 2. 16–18).

How far is this use of the word 'body' metaphorical, and how far is it more? The apostle makes it perfectly clear that what he is speaking of is *not* a natural body but a spiritual body. We shall have to return to this point. But what, precisely, is a 'spiritual body'? In the first place, we are not dealing here simply with the ordinary metaphor by which we ascribe a sort of corporate personality to a group of people organised for some common purpose. That meaning is precluded by the crucial words 'of Christ'—taken in the context of Paul's whole understanding of what Christ has done for us. 'Know ye not that your bodies are members of Christ?' he says, writing to the Corinthians on the subject of fornication. 'Shall I take away the members of Christ, and make them members of a harlot?' (I Cor. 6. 15). In the light of the biblical teaching that sexual intercourse makes of a man and a woman one flesh, nothing could express more violently the almost physical relationship of the believer to Christ in one body. Almost—but not quite; for the relationship is not after the flesh but after the Spirit. He that is joined to the Lord is, not one flesh, but one spirit (I Cor. 6. 17). But that does not mean that the unity is not corporal. It is your bodies—he says—which are members of Christ, and therefore cannot be joined to a harlot. To say that your body is a member of Christ obviously means something much more than saying, 'You are a member of the Christian society,' in the ordinary sense of such a phrase in modern speech. It can only be understood in the light of Paul's teaching that Christ is the life of believers.

We may further test the strength of Paul's language by examining what he says about the factions in the Church at Corinth. When he hears that the Corinthians are beginning to call themselves by the names of rival party leaders, including his own, he expresses his horror and astonishment in a series of very violent phrases: 'Is Christ divided? was Paul crucified for you? or were you baptised into the name of Paul?' (I Cor. 1. 13). These rhetorical questions show how any breach in the unity of the Church was in violent contradiction to the very heart of the Gospel as Paul understood it. To be baptised is to be baptised into Christ and made a member of Him; more precisely, it is to be baptised into His death, to be crucified with Him in order that we may also be members in His risen body. There is only one Christ, and He has only one body. For His members to be divided from one another is to divide Christ. For Christians to call themselves by any other name than His is to suggest the blasphemous absurdity that Paul or some other human leader was crucified for them. Such associations of Christians in the name of some human leader are of the flesh, not of the Spirit. They are carnal, and those who belong to them walk not as members of Christ but as men. The spiritual life is life in the one body of Christ, and all faction is contradictory of its very nature. There can be several 'bodies of Christians' in the modern sense of the word 'body'. But there can only be one body of Christ, and the Christian life is life in that body.

In St. Paul's treatment of the Lord's Supper in this epistle, the same point becomes clear (chapters 10 and 11). The common sharing in the one loaf and the one cup, which is the visible bond of union among them, is nothing less than a communion, a participation, in the body and blood of Christ. It makes them one body—His body. Therefore, 'You cannot drink the cup of the Lord and the cup of demons.' And therefore also division at the Lord's table must bring down judgment. It makes those guilty of it guilty of the body and blood of the Lord, of rending afresh His body. Their bodies, which have become members of Christ, fall under the power of disease and death, because they eat and drink 'not discerning the body'—in a manner which denies their common membership in Christ.

In the following chapters (chapters 12, 13 and 14) the nature of the common life in the body of Christ is unfolded in relation to the various gifts of the Spirit. Here it is made clear that the correlate of the one Spirit is the one body whose many members have diverse functions but are yet one body. The reference is not to some ideal and invisible entity; nor is it primarily to the universal society of believers, though the passage is relevant to that. The primary reference is to the ordinary daily life of the Christian brotherhood in Corinth. What is described is the life of an actual congregation, a congregation whose life was marked by all the grievous sins of which the apostle has to speak in the earlier chapters. To this congregation he writes: 'Ye are the body of Christ' (12. 27). The same baptism by which they became sharers in the Spirit is that by which they became members in the body. The whole language of the chapter precludes the possibility of separating these from one another and making one prior to the other. 'In one spirit were we all baptised into one body, whether Jews or Greeks, whether bond or free; and were all made to drink of one spirit' (12. 13).

We may summarise this Pauline teaching by saying that the Christian life is life in the body of Christ, a life which involves the identification of ourselves with His death and resurrection, in faith, baptism, and the Lord's Supper. The body of Christ, of which we are thus made members, is not a natural body. But neither, on the other hand, is it an ideal body separable from the actual visible life of the Christian fellowship in the world. It is a spiritual body, the body of Christ—the last Adam who has become a life-giving Spirit. This life-giving spiritual power is now at work in us quickening our mortal bodies. Thereby, though the outward man is decaying, the new, inward man in us is being renewed day by day, while we wait for the consummation, the resurrection of the body wherein what is mortal will be swallowed up in life. Our bodies are even now made members of Christ, and His body thus functions through the mutually interdependent service of the members in the ordinary life of the Church, through preaching, prophecy, teaching, miracles, healing, and so on. The visible centre of this common life is the common sharing in the Lord's Supper, in which the members are made participants in His body and blood. For Christians to find other centres of common life than Him, to call themselves by other names than His, and to fall apart from one another in factions, is a monstrous absurdity, and in such circumstances the Lord's Supper will be an instrument of judgment upon them. The sacrament in such circumstances will not build up the body, but destroy it.

II

The above summary of biblical evidence makes, of course, no pretence at being precise or complete, but it will serve to remind you of the great mass of material from which it is taken. That our Lord spent the days of His flesh primarily in choosing, training and sending forth a fellowship which was to represent Him in the world; that this is in accordance with the whole pattern of the biblical record whose centre is the story of a people; that this is in turn congruous with the biblical teaching that God deals with men as social wholes and not only as individuals; that this in turn rests upon the whole biblical view of the natural world, and of man as a psycho-somatic unity; that the central place given in the Gospel story to the sacraments of baptism and the Lord's Supper is congruous with this teaching; that Paul's use of the phrase 'the body of Christ' involves a conception of our membership in Christ which is essentially membership in one undivided visible fellowship: these things at least are clear from the New Testament. We may now go on to remind ourselves of elements in the long story of the Church which have, so to say, underlined the truth in these biblical affirmations.

1. We may point first of all to the testimony which church history bears to the fact that the Church cannot live except as a visibly defined and organised body with a continuing structure. It is not necessary, I think, to illustrate this by a great many examples. We can all call to mind movements which have begun as pure upsurges of fresh spiritual vitality, breaking through and revolting against the hardened structure of the older body, and claiming, in the name of the Spirit, liberty from outward forms and institutions. And we have seen how rapidly they develop their own forms, their own structures of thought, of language, and of organisation. It would surely be a very unbiblical view of human nature and history to think—as we so often, in our pagan way, do—that this is just an example of the tendency of all things to slide down from a golden age to an age of iron, to identify the spiritual with the disembodied, and to regard visible structure as equivalent to sin. We must rather recognise here a testimony to

the fact that Christianity is, in its very heart and essence, not a disembodied spirituality, but life in a visible fellowship, a life which makes such total claim upon us, and so engages our total powers, that nothing less than the closest and most binding association of men with one another can serve its purpose. And moreover it belongs to the very essence of the Christian religion that the fellowship into which it binds us embraces all men and all generations, and therefore every association of Christians which claims to be the Church necessarily tends to develop the traditional marks of structure and succession, even though it has begun in a revolt against tradition. Things which are repudiated in the act of breaking away are reasserted in the practical business of Church life a generation later. The difficulty is that while the act of breaking away is defended by an explicit theology, the day-by-day developments of Church life escape the scrutiny of the theologian, and their significance is missed. Thus the same Luther who denied in principle that the Church could exclude him from the communion of Christ, in later life placed the use of the power of the keys among the essential marks of the Church alongside of the word and sacraments. The followers of Calvin and Knox, who had both absolutely denied that ministerial succession is a mark of the true Church, are found asserting a perpetual succession of presbyters. And the followers of John Wesley, who had performed an act of ordination for which he had no ecclesiastical authority, would probably be more horrified than any other body of Christians if one of their members today did the same. These things are not signs of the inconstancy of the nature of man, but precisely signs of a certain constancy which God has written into the constitution of man and into the constitution of His Church. They are a deeply impressive testimony to the fact that it belongs to the nature of the Church to have a visible and continuing structure. In the New Testament that structure is expressed in very simple terms—continuance in the apostles' teaching and fellowship, the breaking of bread and the prayers. Even our perversions and caricatures of that structure, even the appalling modern development of church bureaucracy which perhaps most afflicts the Churches which have most tried to deny that church order belongs to the substance of the Christian religion, all bear witness to the fact that being in Christ means being incorporated in a visible society which is—in principle—

undivided and continuous, binding all men and all generations in the one body of Christ, from His coming until His coming again.

2. In the second place, does not church history compel us to confess that when something else has been put in the place of this structure, something very important has been lost? I speak here with the greatest hesitation, for I realise that a vast amount of historical learning and wisdom which I do not possess would be needed to justify the assertion that I am making. I am myself wholly persuaded that there have been, and may be again, occasions when a break in the continuing structure is—under the conditions created by human sin—inevitable if the truth of the Gospel is to be maintained. When the Church becomes corrupt and its message distorted, God does raise up prophets to speak His word afresh, and groups in whom His Spirit brings forth afresh His authentic fruits. When these new gifts can be assimilated within the old structure they serve to renew it all. But when a break occurs and a new structure is formed upon the basis of the particular doctrine of the reformer, or the particular spiritual experience of the group, something essential to the true being of the Church has been lost. The body which results is inevitably shaped by the limitations which mark even the greatest individual minds. It necessarily lacks the richness and completeness which belongs to the whole catholic Church. As we have already seen, it will inevitably begin at once to develop its own structure. But this structure will be derivative and not primary. The primary thing will be a doctrine or an experience. But this means that structure will be related to faith and experience in a way fundamentally different from the way they are related in the New Testament. Here we do not find that our Lord first laid down a compendium of doctrine and then invited those who believed it to form an association on that basis. The personal fellowship and the doctrine were given together, and in such wise that in both there was room for ever-new growth. The divine society into which He admitted men was more than a school of correct theology. It was a personal fellowship of those who believed in Him, who had yet many things to learn which they would only learn slowly and stumblingly, but who could be trusted to be His ambassadors to the world and the foundation stones of His Church because they abode in Him. To them He gave no authorised creed. The boundaries of His society were not to be fixed by

subscription to a precisely formulated theology. He gave them the two sacraments of His death and resurrection by which His visible society would be defined. And within these limits they would have the perfect freedom of the Spirit who would lead them into all the truth. In one sense these limits are rigid. This rigidity is of the essence of the sacraments, but it is precisely this rigidity which makes freedom possible, just as the rigidity of the rules of grammar makes freedom of speech possible. I think it must be frankly admitted that when, in the name of a purer faith or a richer experience, Christians have felt compelled to break with the continuing structure, and have therefore claimed a primacy for faith or experience over order, their children and grandchildren have inherited from them new structures based upon some particular formulation of faith or experience which have allowed less spiritual and intellectual freedom than that which the reformers took for granted. In the New Testament faith and order are given together. When, because of sin, situations arise where men apparently have to choose between them, and faith is given a theoretical primacy over order, the eventual result is a new order based upon a particular and partial formulation of faith, and the new order is inevitably less free, because less catholic, than the old. It is perhaps needless to say that this may and almost certainly will apply to both sides of the rift, and that when order is given priority over faith the effect is equally disastrous.

3. A third element in church history which may be said to underline the truth of the position we are discussing is what one must describe as the whittling away of the sacraments at many times and places in Protestant history. I think it is not necessary to enlarge on this. We have known forms of church life in which the sacraments were apparently mere signs, ancient customs to be preserved but not organs on which the Church depended for its very life; in which baptism was sentimentalised into a touching family occasion, a little piece of sanctified baby-worship, with all the real biblical teaching about dying with Christ and being regenerate in Him dissolved away; in which it did not really matter afterwards whether a man had been baptised or not; in which the Lord's Supper was little more than an impressive illustration of the sermon, something that the Church could do without and still be much the same. I mention this merely to

remind you that when this happens the Church becomes some-thing very different from what is given in the New Testament. When we allow ourselves to be more rational or more spiritual than Christ who gave us these two sacraments, we violate the nature which God has given us, and take upon ourselves more than we were meant to bear. When we claim to possess a religion so spiritual that we can see past these visible signs to their mean-ing, and therefore can dispense with them, the inevitable result is that we lose a certain simplicity and a certain awareness of ulti-mate mystery which belong to the very heart of man's true response to God. Seeking to rise above the ordinary limitations of humanity we become something less than human. What God has done for us in Christ, what we have to rely on, is much more than we can formulate in detailed statements or appropriate in conscious religious experience. The heart of our life in Christ must therefore be a sort of casting of ourselves upon those visible and tangible assurances which He has given us. He *has* sent forth His Church, given to it His Spirit, and furnished it with these visible and tangible means of His presence. Even the wisest must in the end become as a little child and accept what He has given, ever seeking to enter more fully into its meaning, yet ever know-ing that the reality infinitely exceeds that part of it which he has grasped.

4. This is related to a fourth point which deserves mention. In attacks upon the Catholic position it is common to lay stress upon the fact that the relationship which God establishes with us in Christ is a purely personal relationship, constituted wholly by grace on His side and faith on ours, and that consequently imper-sonal and institutional conceptions must not be allowed to play a decisive part in our thinking about the Church. From this point of view both the sacraments and the institutional life of the Church are regarded as something less than central in the life of the Christian. In some statements of this view, the Church becomes merely a sort of framework within which such a true personal relationship between God and the souls of men, and between men and men, may develop, but which is purely instru-mental to this purpose and to be altered, discarded, or replaced as the fulfilment of this purpose requires. To those who hold this view, insistence upon the use of sacraments as essential to the being of the Church seems intolerable, and the doctrine that my

relationship to Christ should be affected by the historic continuity or discontinuity of the Church to which I belong quite incredible. The exploration of the meaning of personal relationship is one of the great achievements of thought in our time, and one that has been immensely helpful in the understanding of the Christian faith. But is it not necessary also to insist that all personal relationships are given to us in an impersonal context and conditioned by impersonal factors? Is it not significant that the deepest, most fruitful, and most satisfying personal relationships are those in which the impersonal factors are at their maximum, in which the personal is most indissolubly connected with physical, biological and economic factors—namely in marriage and the family? And must we not assert that the attempt to isolate the personal, and to set it over against the legal and institutional, does violence to its nature? Must one not say that the attempt, in the conditions of human nature, to have a personal relation divorced from its proper impersonal context is futile? It is surely congruous with the whole nature of man that Christ, in giving us Himself, has given us a Church which is His body on earth and therefore marked by visible limits and a continuing structure, so that fellowship with Him should be by incorporation in it.

III

We conclude that, just as it belongs to the heart of the biblical doctrine of the Church that our incorporation in Christ is by faith, so it is no less central to this doctrine that our incorporation is by baptism into a visible fellowship which is the body of Christ in Corinth, in Rome, in the world; and that our participation in the life of the body is maintained by our sharing in the one loaf and the one cup in one undivided fellowship. The Church, in other words, is not constituted by a series of disconnected human responses to the supernatural acts of divine grace in the word and sacraments. It is the continuing life of Christ among men in a body which grows by the addition of new members but is itself essentially continuous and indivisible. There is but one Christ and therefore but one body of Christ, growing up in all things into Him the Head, one holy temple built upon the foundation of apostles and prophets, Christ Jesus Himself being the chief cornerstone, and growing up into a holy temple in the Lord. Its unity is not merely ideal or spiritual: it is visible, social, organic; effected, revealed, and sealed in the fellowship of the one table. Breach of that fellowship makes the sacrament into an instrument of judgment. Disunity in the Church is no mere external crack on the surface of a solid reality. It is something which goes down to its very core.

The natural result of unity will be continuity in the transmission of authority. Here also a breach is something which involves the very heart of the life of the Church. We are not here speaking of the continuity of Christian experience or of teaching. That also is a fact of central importance to the life of the Church. But we are here speaking of something more precise and definable. As long as the body remains one, its authority will be transmitted in orderly succession from generation to generation. Only if there is a schism will there be a breach in that succession, and in place of one ministerial succession there will be two, the second dating from the point at which the schism occurred. How, then, are we to interpret what has happened when such a breach occurs? If it be true, as we are asserting, that it belongs to the essence of the Church to be one indivisible and continuing fellowship, the conclusion seems close at hand that the body which has lost the succession has thereby lost the right to call itself the Church. And in that case it avails nothing that it possesses the sacraments, for they will be instruments not of grace but of judgment. It would seem that such bodies ought simply to sicken and die. And we must remember that some do. There are examples of precisely such schisms in which the separated body has no principle of life in it and simply decays. But manifestly that is not true of all. No one who is not spiritually blind or worse can fail to acknowledge that God has signally and abundantly blessed the preaching, sacraments and ministry of great bodies which can claim no uninterrupted ministerial succession from the apostles, but who have contributed at least as much as those who have remained within it to the preaching of the Gospel, the conversion of sinners, and the building up of the saints in holiness. Any theology which tries in any way to evade the most complete acknowledgment of that fact is self-condemned. Like the Church in Jerusalem listening to Paul and Barnabas, we must at this point simply be silent and hearken to what God has done.

Nor can we attempt to preserve some remnants of consistency

by the use of the conception of uncovenanted mercies, by suggesting that we can acknowledge fully the works of grace outside of the visible Church and yet retain intact our conviction that the Church only exists where visible continuity has been preserved. This attempt lands us into an impossible situation. If God can and does bestow His redeeming grace with indiscriminate bounty within and without the confines of His Church, then the Church is no essential part of the whole scheme of salvation, and its order and sacraments, its preaching and ministering have no inherent and essential relation to God's saving work in Christ, but are mere arbitrary constructions which God Himself ignores. Of course no Christian would accept such a view for a moment, but it is not often noticed how perilously near to this absurdity we come when we try to salvage a rigid theory of the Church by a too lavish use of the formula *Deus non alligatur sacramentis sed nos*. The Church in the New Testament is that real, visible, human fellowship in which Christ is alive in His members, and they are growing up into Him. Those who seek Him must find Him there and nowhere else, for the world—as over against the Church—lieth in the evil one. I do not think that it is possible to deny that the Church, so understood, exists in bodies which have lost the visible succession.

But, if this assertion is true, where is the flaw in the reasoning that seemed to force us so inescapably to the conclusion that the Church can exist only where the succession has continued unbroken? The answer, of course, is to be found precisely in that truth which St. Paul sets forth in the Epistle to Romans, in meeting the same problem as it was posed by the relation of the Church to the Synagogue. It is that God's people have their standing before Him, their participation in His divine life, solely by grace through faith; that the Church exists always and only by His sheer, unmerited mercy—the mercy of Him who raises the dead, justifies the sinner, and calls the things that are not as though they were. The fundamental flaw in the position we are examining is that it forgets that the substance of the covenant is pure mercy, and that God retains His sovereign freedom to have mercy upon whom He will, and to call 'No people' His people when they that are called His people deny their calling by unbelief and sin.

But does the Church, as such, sin? We must begin by asking

this question because it takes us to the heart of our criticism of the Catholic position. The Church (it is said), the body of Christ, the extension of the incarnation, is God's instrument of redemption holding out to all men the means of deliverance from sin. It has His promise that the gates of hell shall not prevail against it. As such it does not sin, but on the contrary carries with it the means of grace by which sin in its members is purged away and they are schooled in holiness. This is the characteristic Catholic teaching. And if this be true, it would certainly seem to follow that there can be no circumstance in which a separation from the Church's fellowship is justifiable, and therefore no separated body which can hope for the blessing of God. And it would also follow that, while we might speak of the standing of the individual before God in terms of faith answering free grace, these would not be the proper terms in which to describe the life of the Church. But is it true? Let us begin with what is agreed: that the Church is a real incorporation of men in the life of the risen Christ, in such wise that His life is in them and theirs in Him. It is a real communication of the life of Jesus to men. I repeat the word 'real' in order to deny that it is merely imputed or merely promised. The Church is thus truly spoken of as the body of Christ. But it is important to stress the point that it is *not* truly spoken of as 'the extension of the Incarnation'. That phrase springs from a confusion of *sarx* with *soma*. Christ's risen body is not fleshly but spiritual. He did not come to incorporate us in His body according to the flesh but according to the Spirit. That is why He told His disciples that it was expedient for them that He should go away. The Spirit could not come until His offering up of Himself in the flesh had been completed (John 16. 7; cf. John 7. 39). The 'likeness of sinful flesh' (Rom. 8. 3), in which He came for our sakes, had to be put off, had to fall into the earth and die, had to be offered up, in order that our redemption might be accomplished. Our incorporation in Him is only possible because, having triumphantly done this, He has ascended to His Father and sent forth the Spirit. Our incorporation into His risen life is first of all our incorporation into His death, and this profound paradox governs every part of the Church's life. The Church only lives through dying. The moment its life becomes equated with the natural life of which death is the mere negation—life 'according to the flesh'—it is dead even though it has 'a name that it liveth' (Rev. 3. 1). The Church lives—here on earth—'in the flesh', but its life in Christ is not 'according to the flesh'.

The Church on earth is therefore in a state of warfare. Life according to the flesh and life according to the Spirit struggle in her against one another. The flesh lusts against the Spirit, and the Spirit against the flesh. We are familiar with this conflict in the life of the individual believer. But no believer is a mere individual, and it is surely quite wrong to deny that the same conflict goes on in the life of the Church. Catholic theologians generally feel themselves bound to hold the view that since the Church is the body of Christ it cannot sin. Various ways of escape are suggested from the intolerable absurdity which the contrary admission seems to involve. The Church's 'empirical manifestation', it is said, 'may often belie her true essence' (Mascall). Or it is said that while her members sin, the Church as such is free from sin, and has—in the sacrament of penance—the means of dealing with the sins of her members. But these suggestions really evade the problem. No honest person can deny that the Church as a visible institution has in the course of its history been guilty of pride, greed, sloth and culpable blindness. Nor can we admit the possibility of easing the difficulty by making a radical distinction between the Church and its members. The 'individual Christian' is such only as a member of Christ, and there is no meaning in saying that the body of Christ cannot sin but His members can. Nor, finally, does the New Testament leave us in any doubt that the Church *does* sin. The words, 'Ye are the body of Christ' and the words 'Ye are yet carnal', were addressed by the same apostle to the same body of men and women. The living Lord of the Church can say to a Church, 'I know thy works, that thou hast a name that thou livest, and thou art dead.' The Lord Himself can remove the candlestick out of its place.

Admittedly no rational explanation can be given of the fact that the Church, which is the Body of Christ, may sin. But only harm can come of denying a fact so plainly attested. We cannot explain evil in the Church or in ourselves. We cannot understand why the prince of this world whom Christ cast out of his usurped dominion by His victory on the Cross should still have power over us. The darkness of that perplexity only becomes bearable when it is illuminated by the eschatological hope. And conversely it is the removal of that hope which leads men into the error of

F

denying the fact of sin in the Church. We shall have to speak
more about this matter later, for it is central to our theme. Meanwhile it is enough to say that the life of the new man in Christ
is *both* a reality now given, *and* a reality whose completeness
awaits the day of Christ's return. In this time 'between the times',
we are made one in Him by the Spirit—and the Spirit is the spirit
of promise, the earnest, the foretaste of the completed victory
of God. It is the mark of human life 'after the flesh', that is human
life in its separation from God, that it seeks to have its fullness in
itself as a present possession. It is the mark of life after the Spirit
that it looks always to God in dependence and hope. It longs for
the day of God's victory and places all its confidence in that.
Under the conditions of the flesh, the victory of God is known
only as defeat. The sign of the Cross is the sign under which the
Church must ever live in the flesh. When the Church, in the
flesh, under the conditions of this present age, claims to have *in
itself* the completeness of God's victory and therefore to be
incapable of sin, it becomes precisely 'of the flesh'—carnal. The
true mark of the Church's life in the flesh is the mark of the
Cross, of life through death, of 'bearing about in the body the
dying of Jesus, that the life also of Jesus may be manifested in
our body' (II Cor. 4. 10). When, on the other hand, the
Church is identified simply with whatever society has continued
in unbroken institutional succession from the time of the apostles,
then the flesh, not the Spirit, has been made determinative. There
is in truth no 'extension of the Incarnation', for His incarnation
was in order to make an offering of Himself in the flesh 'once
for all'. The fruit of that offering, of that casting of a corn of
wheat into the earth, is the extension of His risen life to all who
are made members of His Body in the one Spirit—until He comes
again.

The fundamental error into which Catholic doctrines of the
Church are prone to fall is (as William Nicholls has shown with
great clarity)[1] the error of subordinating the eschatological to the
historical. Of course no theology which is bound to the Scriptures
and the Creeds can formally deny the faith in Christ's coming
again, but the point is that what we may call the 'atmosphere' of
the New Testament, in which faith and love are known only in
an indissoluble unity with hope, is lost. The Church is treated

---

[1] *Ecumenism and Catholicity*, Wm. Nicholls.

as having, for practical purposes, the whole plenitude of God's grace in itself now. God has, as it were, deposited His grace with the Church and left 'it' to her to administer. The hymn sung in so many Churches on Ember days expresses precisely this idea:

> 'So age by age, and year by year,
> His grace was handed on;
> And still the holy Church is here
> Although her Lord is gone.'

The Church seems here to have become a purely historical institution, the trustee of an absent landlord. I do not wish to deny the element of truth in the doctrine. It is true that the Lord calls upon us to be faithful in that which He has entrusted to us until He comes. We are made stewards of His grace and shall be answerable for our stewardship on the day of His appearing. But it is not true that the Church possesses *in herself* the plenitude of His grace. Such a phrase as that of St. Paul, 'We through the Spirit by faith wait for the hope of righteousness,' and many others like it, remind us of the completely different 'atmosphere' of New Testament Christianity. The Church lives in the Spirit by faith, and each of these words is shot through and through with the tension of hope. The Spirit is the *arrabon*, the foretaste which assures us of God's grace and yet makes us long for it because we know how far we are from grace. Faith is the substance of things hoped for, the evidence of things not seen. It rises out of what is not, to grasp what is and shall be. The whole passion of Paul's polemic against the circumcision party, his warning that those who are circumcised will be severed from Christ, his blunt assertion that the desire for circumcision is simply a desire 'to make a fair show in the flesh', his reiterated insistence upon faith and hope as against the works of the law, are all relevant to the issue we are here considering. The very mark of the flesh, in the biblical sense of the word, is the desire to have something of one's own apart from God. When the Church claims to have the plenitude of grace in itself, it has abandoned the Spirit for the flesh. It is truly the body of Christ when it is truly spiritual, living in faith, knowing that it has and is nothing in itself, but lives only in ardent longing and eager receptiveness, ever ready to confess that God alone is good and to ascribe all glory and wisdom to Him.

In fact the Church has sinned, and—in the new dispensation as in the old—God retains His freedom over His Church to chastise and correct, to call those who were no people His people, to raise up of the stones children of Abraham. He is faithful to His covenant even when men are unfaithful, but the whole purpose of His covenant is—as St. Paul makes so clear—that He may have mercy upon all. Therefore there can be no room in it for any human claim upon God, for any thought that whereas those outside the covenant must depend simply on the free and un-covenanted mercy of God, those within it have—as it were—a *right* to His mercy. We have already pointed out that the complexity of Paul's argument in Romans 9–11 arises from just this fact. There is a covenant and a covenant people, and God is faithful to His covenant. But the substance of that covenant is all pure mercy and grace. If men presume to claim for themselves upon the basis of the covenant some relationship with God other than that of the sinner needing God's grace, the covenant has been perverted. And where that has happened God, in the sovereign freedom of His grace, destroys these pretensions, calls 'No people' to be the people, breaks off natural branches and grafts in wild slips, filling them with the life which is His own life imparted to men. There is no law in His Kingdom save the law of pure grace. That is why they come from east and west to sit down with Abraham and Isaac, while the sons of the Kingdom are cast out, for the sons of the Kingdom have no place there unless they are willing to sit down with all whom the Lord of the feast shall call, and to receive His mercy in exactly the same way as the publicans and sinners.

From its very beginnings the Church faces us with the dark mystery of sin by which she lives and acts in a manner that con-tradicts her essential nature. She who is essentially one is divided; she who is essentially holy is unclean; she who is essentially apostolic forgets her missionary task. No doctrine of the Church can be true which does not match this dark mystery of sin in the Church with a doctrine of the divine grace profound enough to deal with it without evasion, and which does not in some measure explain how a body which by sin denies its own nature is yet accepted by God and used as the means of His grace. I have sought to show that the Church's unity and continuity are of its *esse* and cannot be treated as secondary and dispensable elements in its life.

But it is no less of the *esse* of the Church that it should be holy, and that it should be apostolic, which I take to mean both holding the apostolic faith and prosecuting the apostolic mission to the world. A Church which denies any of these elements in its life denies its essential being. Having done so, it can exist as a Church only by the sheer grace and mercy of God. Holiness and apostolicity belong, equally with unity, to the essence of the Church. What seems to be implied in so-called Catholic definitions of the Church, however, is that while a Church may in other matters lose what belongs to its essence and yet be accepted by God as a Church, a Church which loses its continuity with the undivided Church forfeits completely its character as part of the Catholic Church; that though a Church be besotted with corruption, bound to the world in an unholy alliance, rent with faction, filled with false teaching, and utterly without missionary zeal, God's mercy is big enough to cover these defects and they do not therefore destroy its claim to be regarded as part of the Church; but that though a Church be filled with all the fruits of the Holy Spirit, if it lack the apostolic succession it is no part of the Church and all the mercy of God is not enough to make it so.

In what I have just said I have put the point bluntly and perhaps therefore unfairly. Many Catholics are eager to acknowledge that baptised members of Christian bodies outside of the visible unity of the Church as defined by them are yet in some sense members of the Church, and even that these bodies are in some sense Churches. It is even suggested that there are degrees of membership in the Church, some bodies being in the centre and possessing all the plenitude of 'churchliness', and others at varying distances, until on the far horizons one discerns presumably the Quakers, the Salvation Army, and the Plymouth Brethren. But I can only say that I cannot fit such ideas into the framework of New Testament thought. I do not mean to advocate a mere relativism, to suggest that the form of the Church simply does not matter. I hope I have already shown sufficient grounds for the belief that the form of the Church matters a great deal, that the unity of the Church, and therefore its continuity, is of its *esse*, and that the subordination of order to faith is not in accordance with the teaching of the New Testament. With regard to what the Church ought to be, I think we have every ground to insist that our Lord has given us very clear directions indeed. But with regard to what we are, I think we must simply say that God has concluded all under sin that He may have mercy on all. In other words I think that we are here dealing with the same fundamental paradox as in the discussion of law and grace in the Epistles to Romans and Galatians. The Catholic is right in insisting that the continuity of the Church is God's will. He is wrong when he suggests that the doing of that will is the condition of our standing in His grace. As for the individual, so also for the Church, there is only one way to be justified, and it is to say, 'God be merciful to me a sinner.'

IV

THE COMMUNITY OF
THE HOLY SPIRIT

CATHOLICISM and orthodox Protestantism, however deeply they have differed from one another, have been at one in laying immense stress on that in the Christian religion which is given and unalterable. Catholicism has laid its primary stress upon the given structure, Protestantism upon the given message, but both have known, at their best, that in so doing they were seeking to honour and safeguard the uniqueness, sufficiency and finality of God's saving acts in Christ. Within the context of the modern ecumenical movement representatives of these two streams of Christian faith and practice have come increasingly to recognise that this is so, and to acknowledge that, in spite of the deep differences between them, they are seeking to be faithful to the same truth. It is necessary, however, to recognise that there is a third stream of Christian tradition which, though of course mingling at many points with the other two, has yet a distinct character of its own. It is important to recognise this fact because this stream at present runs more outside of, than inside of, the ecumenical movement, and has so far taken an inadequate part in the theological encounter which that movement has made possible.

Let me in a brief and preliminary way characterise this stream by saying that its central element is the conviction that the Christian life is a matter of the experienced power and presence of the Holy Spirit today; that neither orthodoxy of doctrine nor impeccability of succession can take the place of this; that an excessive emphasis upon those immutable elements in the Gospel upon which orthodox Catholicism and Protestantism have concentrated attention may, and in fact often does, result in a Church which is a mere shell, having the form of a Church but not the life; that if we would answer the question 'Where is the Church?', we must ask 'Where is the Holy Spirit recognisably present with power?' Those who belong to this stream of Christian faith and life confront the orthodox Protestant and Catholic alike with words such as George Fox addressed to Margaret Fell: 'What had any to do with the Scriptures, but as they came to the Spirit that gave them forth? You will say, Christ saith this, and the apostles this; but what canst thou say?'—words reminiscent of an earlier and grimmer question: 'Jesus I know and Paul I know, but who are ye?'

I have admitted that it is difficult to give a single name to this stream of Christian tradition, and that may seem to be an argument against according to it separate treatment. But, on the other hand, although it overlaps with both Catholic and Protestant traditions its distinctiveness is seen in the fact that at some points it agrees with Catholicism against Protestantism, and at others with Protestantism against Catholicism. An obvious example of the latter is its neglect of visible order and structure. As an example of the former, one can point to its strong conviction that the new life in the Spirit is an actually experienced and received reality, something involving an ontological change in the believer. For want of a better word I propose to refer to this type of Christian faith and life as the Pentecostal.

I

The biblical evidence which can be adduced in support of the position which we are now to examine is so abundant that I cannot do more than remind you of a few outstanding groups of passages. We may begin by again referring to the receiving of the first Gentile converts, and Peter's reflections thereon. While Peter was still in the midst of his sermon, you will remember, 'the Holy Ghost fell on all them which heard the word. And they of the circumcision which believed were amazed, as many as came with Peter, because that on the Gentiles also was poured out the gift of the Holy Ghost. For they heard them speak with tongues, and magnify God. Then answered Peter, Can any man forbid the water, that these should not be baptised, which have received the Holy Ghost as well as we?' (Acts 10. 44-47). At two later points Peter had occasion to speak about this event before his brethren. When challenged to defend his action his answer was absolutely simple and clear-cut. 'I remembered the

word of the Lord, how that he said, John indeed baptised with
water; but ye shall be baptised with the Holy Ghost. If then God
gave unto them the like gift as he did also unto us, when we believed on the Lord Jesus Christ, who was I, that I could withstand
God? And when they heard these things, they held their peace, and
glorified God, saying, Then to the Gentiles also hath God granted
repentance unto life' (Acts 11. 16–18). Nothing could be more plain
or unambiguous. The gift of the Spirit was a visible, recognisable,
unquestionable sign that God had accepted these Gentiles as His
own people, and before that fact the most massive and fundamental
theological convictions simply had to give way. The Holy Spirit
may be the last article of the Creed but in the New Testament it is
the first fact of experience. We are accustomed to discuss the Holy
Spirit as a doctrine after we have dealt with creation, incarnation,
atonement and so on. In the New Testament the Holy Spirit appears
rather as a sheer fact, God's recognisable witness (e.g. Acts 15. 8)
to His own presence, and therefore entitled to right of way before
all arguments based on an *a priori* reasoning. The repeated use
of the word 'witness' in relation to the Spirit is a reminder of
just this point: the Holy Spirit's presence is the plain fact by which
we know God's mind towards us. 'We are witnesses', say the
apostles, when challenged to show their authority, 'and so is
the Holy Ghost, whom God hath given to them that obey him'
(Acts 5. 32). The question, 'Have you received the Holy Ghost?',
is one that admits of a plain answer (Acts 19. 1–7; cf. 8. 14–17),
and 'if any man hath not the Spirit of Christ, he is none of his'
(Rom. 8. 9). When Paul argues with the Galatians about law and
faith, he asks them: 'This only would I learn from you, Received
ye the Spirit by the works of the law, or by the hearing of faith?
Are ye so foolish? having begun in the Spirit, are ye now perfected in the flesh?' (Gal. 3. 2–3). When everything is in confusion
and the harassed apostle seeks a firm starting-point for his argument, a fact which all will acknowledge at once, he finds it in
this: the receiving of the Spirit was the starting-point of their
Christian life. Once more we see that the Holy Spirit is not the
end of an argument but the fact from which argument can begin.
In just the same way John can write: 'We know that he abideth
in us, by the Spirit which he gave us' (I John 3. 24), and again:
'Hereby know we that we abide in him, and he in us, because
he hath given us of his Spirit' (I John 4. 13). The Holy Spirit is

the Church's life. Those who lie to the Church, lie to the Holy Spirit (Acts 5. 3). The Holy Spirit is party to the decisions of a Church Council (Acts 15. 28). The Church is, in the most exact sense, a *koinonia*, a common sharing in the Holy Spirit.

Peter, defending his action at Caesarea before his brethren, reminds them of what had happened on the day of Pentecost. 'The Holy Spirit fell on them, even as on us at the beginning.' On that day we may say that everything was ready for the Church's life to begin. Christ's atoning work had been completed. His revelation of the Father in word and deed was complete. The nucleus of His Church was chosen and ready. Speaking in the terms of our earlier argument we may say that both the message and the structure, both faith and order, were complete. And yet, they had to wait. All was complete: and yet nothing was complete until the Spirit of God Himself should be breathed into the new race of men. Only then, empowered by Him, could they go forth to proclaim the message of salvation, and to baptise men in the Name of Christ unto remission of their sins. In very truth it is the presence of the Holy Spirit that constitutes the Church.

It is impossible to give more than the briefest summary of the immense mass of biblical material bearing on this indissoluble connection between the Holy Spirit and the Church. The Holy Spirit is the seal by whom we are sealed unto the day of redemption (Eph. 1. 13; 4. 30; II Cor. 1. 22), in whom we have the foretaste, the earnest, the first fruits of the new age. It is thus in virtue of our having received the Spirit that we are living in the new age, and that the powers of the age to come work in us (e.g. Acts 2. 17–21, 33; Rom. 8. 11, 23; Heb. 6. 4–5; cf. Gal. 5. 5). The Spirit is thus the 'witness' to the Lordship of Jesus, a witness both to the believer and to the world (Acts 5. 32; 15. 3; John 15. 26; 16. 13–14; I John 5. 7; Heb. 2. 4; I Cor. 12. 3). He is called the Spirit of adoption (Rom. 8. 15) because it is only in the Spirit that we are made sons of God, and able to cry to Him as Father. He is the agent of the new, supernatural birth by which we are made sons of God, born after the Spirit in contrast to those who are born after the flesh and therefore trust in the law (Gal. 4. 29; cf. John 3. 5–6). It is thus in Him that we have access to the Father (Eph. 2. 18). This new life of the Spirit in us is that which brings forth all manner of good fruit (Gal. 5. 22–23) and the tree is to be known by its fruits (Matt. 7. 16–20). This new life will finally overcome the death which is at work in our mortal bodies. It is even now at work in them even while they outwardly decay (Rom. 8. 11; II Cor. 5. 1–5). It is the Spirit who gives power to the words of the Christian preaching, which as mere words can accomplish nothing (I Cor. 2. 4; I Thess. 1. 5; Rom. 15. 19). It is the Spirit who guides the Church in its day-to-day activity (Acts 6. 3), directs its missionary work (Acts 8. 29; 10. 19–20; 16. 6–8), supplies all the differing gifts which are required for its common life (I Cor. 12. 4–30; Phil. 1. 19), and leads it into all the truth (John 16. 13). It is the Spirit who rules over the Church's worship and fellowship (I Cor. 14). And the Spirit Himself gives the spiritual sight by which He is to be discerned. It is the Spirit who searches the deep things of God and gives us knowledge of them because we have received that Spirit who is the very Spirit of God. It is He who enables us to recognise what God has given us. This knowledge is unintelligible to the natural man, because the things of the Spirit are spiritually judged, and can only be interpreted to those in whom the Spirit dwells (I Cor. 2. 10–16). To sum up, to be in Christ is to share in His anointing, to have that Spirit by whom the word was made flesh (Luke 1. 35) and by whom the incarnate Word was anointed that He might fulfil the mission for which He was sent (Luke 3. 21–22; Acts 10. 38); it is to have 'an anointing from the Holy One' (I John 2. 20). And this anointing is nothing doubtful or debatable; on the contrary, it is the sure fact upon which we can rest our confidence that we are in Him and He in us: 'Hereby we know that he abideth in us, by the Spirit which he gave us' (I John 3. 24).

Theologians today are afraid of the word 'experience'. There are some good reasons for this, and also some bad ones. But I do not think it is possible to survey this New Testament evidence, even in the most cursory way in which we have done, without recognising that the New Testament writers are free from this fear. They recount happenings which we would subsume under the head of religious experience, and do not hesitate to ascribe them to the mighty power of God and to give them right of way in theological argument over long-cherished convictions. They regard the gift of the Holy Spirit as an event which can be unmistakably recognised, and they treat it as the determinative and decisive thing by which the Church is constituted. The living

Spirit incorporates us in Christ, and where He is, there is the life and power of God. His coming replaces the old seal of circumcision by which God's people were formerly marked off from the world. Circumcision is now seen to be an affair of the flesh (Phil. 3. 3; Gal. 6. 12); the new seal is the gift of the Spirit, of a wholly new divine life, which is in fact the life of the risen Christ Himself in those who have died with Him, a true circumcision not made with hands, a circumcision of the heart which marks God's true people (Phil. 3; II Cor. 1. 22; Eph. 1. 13; 4. 30; Col. 2. 11–12; cf. Acts 7. 51). The Holy Spirit is the seal of God's people, the badge of their sonship, and the earnest of their future inheritance.

There is no gainsaying the decisive place given in the New Testament doctrine of the Church to this experienced reality of the Holy Spirit's presence. We may readily acknowledge that the New Testament itself shows a shift of emphasis as the story proceeds; that St. Paul makes it his business to wean his converts from an excessive love of the more spectacular fruits of the Spirit and to direct them to a love of His more normal and abiding fruits. But this in no way destroys the point that a decisive place is given to the experienced reality of His presence. Nothing could be more definite than the Johannine word: 'Hereby know we that we abide in him and he in us, because he hath given us of his Spirit.' I believe that when a prospector first strikes oil there is often a violent eruption of the oil which sometimes bursts into flames and burns for many days before it is brought under control. Later on there will be no room for such displays. The oil will all be pumped through pipes and refineries to its destination, and a desire to go back to the early fireworks will be rightly regarded as infantile. But the early displays did at least prove something: they proved that oil was there; and without this all the pipes and refineries in the world are merely futile. My illustration is a crude one, but it will serve well enough to make the point that what I have called the Pentecostal Christian has the New Testament on his side when he demands first of all of any body of so-called Christians, 'Do you have the Holy Spirit? For without that all your credal orthodoxy and all your historic succession avails you nothing.' To quote again the blunt words of St. Paul: 'If any man hath not the Spirit of Christ, he is none of His.'

It is surely necessary to insist that only by the fullest acknowledgment of this truth do we truly acknowledge the lordship of Christ in His Church. His lordship is not adequately acknowledged if we accord decisive place in our doctrine only to that which He has done once for all, essential as this is. We have also to acknowledge Him as the living Lord carrying on today His saving work through the Holy Spirit. Unless the living Spirit Himself takes the things of Christ and shows them to us, we cannot know them. Unless *He* unites us to the ascended Christ we cannot be united. And He is sovereign and free, not to be enclosed within the walls that men erect. 'The wind bloweth where it listeth, and thou hearest the voice thereof, but knowest not whence it cometh and whither it goeth: so is every one that is born of the Spirit' (John 3. 8). No ecclesiastic is likely to feel any more comfortable with those words than Nicodemus did, but he cannot remove them from the Scriptures. Nor, let me add, can he try to evade their force by trying to separate the Spirit from the Church, to acknowledge cheerfully the liberty of the Spirit to blow where it will, so long as the Church stands four-square and solid on the ground so that—if the phrase may be excused—we've got it where we want it. There is surely no warrant in the New Testament for the dissociation of the Spirit of Christ from the body of Christ. Is it not quite incompatible with the teaching of the New Testament to suppose, for instance, that one can gladly acknowledge that a body of Christians shows the clear marks of the Spirit's presence in them, without being thereby obliged to face the question of their churchly character —to face, in fact, the question of intercommunion? I do not want here to suggest any easy answer to the question of intercommunion. That question cannot be separated from the question of visible reunion, and is distorted when it is so separated. But I want to press very seriously the question whether we are not departing altogether from the New Testament doctrine of the body of Christ if we suppose that to acknowledge the presence of the Spirit of Christ does not involve any acknowledgment of the presence of His body.

II

It will be clear from what I have said that I believe that the Catholic-Protestant debate which has characterised the ecumenical movement needs to be criticised and supplemented from what

I have called the Pentecostal angle, that in fact the debate has to become three-cornered. I think it is clear that the Protestant-Catholic dilemma is seen from this angle to be a false one. This dilemma may be expressed in its simplest terms by saying that, in the Church as we know it, life and message are separated, and therefore the question arises: Which is fundamental? This separation is itself the result of sin. In our Lord Himself there is no such separation. He is Himself the message. He is the Word made flesh. In Him word and deed, message and being are one. When He sent forth His apostles into the world He said to them: 'As the Father hath sent me, even so send I you.' They were to be the continuation of His own redeeming mission, his representatives in the profound sense of the Hebrew word *Shaliah*, having and ministering to the world His own divine power to heal and to forgive. This is the central strand in Catholic conviction—that the Church's very being is the continuation of Christ's redeeming mission in the world. But Christ also said to his apostles: 'Ye shall be my witnesses.' That is the permanently valid truth in Protestantism. Although the Church is the continuation of Christ's redeeming mission, in it being and message are not identical. It is not sufficient for the Church to point to itself and say, Here is the body of the Messiah. It must point beyond itself to Him who is sole Judge and Saviour, both of the Church and of the world. And yet the Church is not *merely* the witness to Christ; it is also the body of Christ. It is not merely the reporter of the divine acts of redemption; it is also itself the bearer of God's redeeming grace, itself a part of the story of redemption which is the burden of its message.

We have already looked at the distortions which occur when either of these two elements is given absolute priority over the other. On the one hand the Church is defined simply as that which bears the apostolic witness: where the true witness is, there is the Church. The final result of this is that the Church comes to be defined, as in orthodox Lutheranism, exclusively in terms of assent to precisely formulated doctrinal statements. On the other hand the Church is defined simply as the continuation of the apostolate: where the apostolic succession is, there is the Church. The final result is that the Church comes to be defined as a corporation perpetuating itself by legally valid means, the trustee of an absent Lord. In both cases the Church becomes something which can be identified by purely natural standards and categories. There may, of course, be differences of opinion in a given situation, but in principle the questions of identity of doctrinal statement and of continuity of succession can be settled in any law court by the ordinary rules of evidence. The question: Where is the Church? can thus—on these premises—be answered without any reference to the presence or absence of the Holy Spirit, without any appeal to that discernment of the spirits which is the Spirit's own gift. The apostle asked the converts of Apollos one question: 'Did ye receive the Holy Spirit when you believed?' and got a plain answer. His modern successors are more inclined to ask either 'Did you believe exactly what we teach?' or 'Were the hands that were laid on you our hands?', and—if the answer is satisfactory—to assure the converts that they have received the Holy Spirit even if they don't know it. There is a world of difference between these two attitudes.

The wholeness of the Church is thus not to be sought for simply in a tension between the two elements which we have roughly characterised as Catholic and Protestant. There is a third term which both of them have tended to forget. When the risen Lord bestowed the apostolic commission upon the Church and empowered it to continue His mission, the very heart of His act lay in the bestowal of the Holy Spirit. 'Jesus therefore said to them again, Peace be unto you: as the Father hath sent me, even so send I you. And when he had said this, he breathed on them, and saith unto them, Receive ye the Holy Ghost: whose soever sins ye forgive, they are forgiven unto them: whose soever sins ye retain, they are retained' (John 20. 21–23). It is as anointed with His Spirit that they are bearers of His commission, and in no other way. In precisely the same way the command to be witnesses to Him is inseparably connected with the gift of the Spirit. 'Ye shall receive power, when the Holy Spirit is come upon you: and ye shall be my witnesses' (Acts 1. 8). Indeed, as we have seen, the Holy Spirit is Himself the primary and essential witness, and it is only His presence in the disciples which makes it possible for them truly to witness to Him.

All thinking about the Church must begin in Him in whom message and being are one—the Word made flesh. That is for-ever decisive for the Church's being. In the Church message and being ought ever to be one. Yet because in fact sin sunders them, it is not enough to hold to one of them; the Church must—as it were—cling tightly to both. She cannot surrender the central affirmations either of the Catholic or of the Protestant. But to have said this is still to have left a vital word unsaid. It is indeed to have omitted what is absolutely decisive, for the Church lives neither by her faithfulness to her message nor by her abiding in one fellowship with the apostles; she lives by the living power of the Spirit of God. It was by the Holy Spirit that the Word took flesh of the Virgin Mary. It is by the Holy Spirit that He has now a new body, a body into which only the Holy Spirit can engraft us. Therefore it is only by the living power of the same Holy Spirit that we can either abide in His fellowship or bear witness to His grace. All that is done without Him is mere counterfeit, an empty shell, having the form of a Church but not its life. We must face the fact that this can happen, that a body may have all the outward form of a Church, and preach the true doctrine of the Church, and yet be dead; and on the other hand, that the living Spirit can and does give His own life to bodies which lack in some manner and measure the fullness of the Church's true order and teaching. And when He does so, when we are confronted with manifest tokens of the Spirit's presence, we must, as the apostles did, accept the fact. We must 'hold our peace and glorify God' (Acts 11. 18; cf. 15. 12). There must be no evasion of this, no talk of 'uncovenanted mercies', no suggestion that we can acknowledge the presence of the Holy Spirit and yet deny the fullest Christian fellowship—as though our church rules were stricter than those of God Himself. Where God has 'made no distinction' (Acts 15. 9) we ought to make none. Those whom God has sealed we may not reject without dishonouring God.

I am aware that these words have dangerously revolutionary implications. I use them because they seem to be demanded by fidelity to the Scriptures. In the latter part of this lecture I shall speak of the distortions which result from isolating this aspect of the Church's life from the whole. Here we must frankly face the fact that there *is* in this teaching a revolutionary element which could be dangerously subversive of our existing ways of thought. Let us admit that it is part of the fallen human nature of ecclesiastics, no less than of others in responsible positions, to desire always criteria of judgment which can be used without making too heavy demands upon the delicate faculty of spiritual discernment, clear-cut rules by which we may hope to be saved from making mistakes, or rather from being obviously and personally responsible for the mistakes. We are uncomfortable without definite principles by which we may guide our steps. We fear uncharted country, and the fanatics of all kinds who, upon the alleged authority of the Holy Spirit, summon us with strident cries in all directions simultaneously. Only those who have never borne the heavy burden of pastoral responsibility will mock at the cautious spirit of the ecclesiastic. But on the other hand let us admit that according to the New Testament we are summoned precisely to the task of 'discerning the spirits'; that it is there taken for granted *both* that the Holy Spirit is free and sovereign, able to work in ways that demand re-thinking of our traditional categories, *and* that He Himself gives to the Church the necessary gifts by which He may be known (e.g. I Cor. 12. 10); that in the ordinary life of the Church—alike at worship and at business— He is truly present and truly soveriegn and that we are called upon to know and acknowledge Him (e.g. I Cor. 12. 4–11); that indeed it is precisely to this freedom of sonship that God has called us in Christ (Gal. 4. 21–5. 1), to a liberty in which we are ruled not by the letter of a written code but by the Holy Spirit Himself (II Cor. 3. 4–6).

Such an admission requires us to take with the utmost seriousness the question of the Church's discerning of the spirits. It is not possible here to discuss this question, which is itself the subject of a large literature. The question involves the relation of the Holy Spirit to reason and conscience, to the Church and its unity, and to the Holy Scriptures, the latter issue involving both the related questions of the inspiration of the writers of Scripture, and the place of Scripture in mediating the guidance of the Holy Spirit to us today. Scripture itself lays down, I think, only one absolutely fundamental principle in the matter: 'Every spirit which confesseth that Jesus Christ is come in the flesh is of God, and every spirit which confesseth not Jesus is not of God' (I John 4. 2–3; I Cor. 12. 3). That still leaves open a wide door for error—as the history of the Church shows. But I am sure that it is vital to insist that the discernment of the Spirit can only come by living in the Spirit; that because there is in truth one Spirit who is Lord and God, He is able to make Himself known as one to those who

G

earnestly seek Him; that all who have ever had any taste of His power to teach, convince and subdue a gathering of Christians coming together with all their clashing wills and affections, know that this is true; and that whenever we try to seek some other sort of security against error and disunity, some criteria of judgment or rules of life which can be operated apart from this discernment of the Spirit in the Spirit, some ecclesiastical order in which we can be secure against error without constantly engaging in the risky adventure of seeking truth, secure against schism without constantly paying the price of unity in costly charity, we are in fact building not according to the Spirit but according to the flesh. We must take simply and seriously the truth that the Church is a communion in the Holy Spirit, and that He is no cypher, no abstract noun, but living Lord.

III

I began this lecture by reminding you that whereas Catholicism and Protestantism have laid immense stress upon what is given and unalterable, the type of Christian faith and life which I have called Pentecostal has laid its stress upon that which is to be known and recognised in present experience—the power of the ever-living Spirit of God. It is not surprising that the errors and distortions which have marked this type of Christian faith and life have been in the direction of isolating the particular truth to which it has borne witness and ignoring that which is given once and for all. In its most extreme form this has led some into a sort of non-historical mysticism in which the work of the Holy Spirit in the heart is regarded as practically independent of Christ's work in the flesh, the Scriptures, and the sacraments. One may presume that the apostolic warning concerning those who claim the Spirit but deny 'Jesus come in the flesh' is directed against early developments of this kind. One can indeed understand how St. Paul's teaching, that even though he has known Christ after the flesh yet now he knows Him so no more, might be thought to lead on to a sort of 'religion of the Holy Spirit' which could leave the incarnation and its consequences behind. The truth of course is, as the New Testament everywhere teaches, that God's gift of the Holy Spirit is inseparably linked by the double bond of word and sacrament to His work of redemption in Christ finished once for all in the time of Pontius Pilate. Men and women become sharers in the communion of the Holy Spirit by hearing and believing the proclamation of what He has done, and by being received through baptism into the visible fellowship which He sent forth. In one Spirit were we all baptised into one body, and equally, we received the Spirit by the hearing of faith. On the one hand, both preaching and baptism are made effective by the Spirit; on the other, they are the means by which alone the finished work of the Anointed One can be communicated to the believer, and by which therefore it becomes possible for him to share in the same anointing. I am aware that I am here passing by detailed problems of interpretation—the problem of the converts in Cornelius' house who received the gift of the Spirit before they were baptised, and of those in Samaria who were baptised but had not received the Spirit. These seem to me to show that there is no absolute and mechanical uniformity of the Spirit's working in these matters. But they do not weaken the massive central witness of the New Testament to the truth that the gift of the Holy Spirit is bound to the finished work of Christ by the twin bonds of hearing and believing the message and being baptised into the fellowship of His death and resurrection. The attempt to sever these bonds by giving anything less than a central place to word and sacraments involves a fundamental departure from the religion of the New Testament.

It is important to state at this point that these bonds are not arbitrary and incomprehensible, but are proper to the whole Gospel of redemption through Jesus Christ. We touch here again that aspect of biblical thought which we referred to in the last lecture. God, according to the Bible, is concerned with the redemption of the whole human race and of the whole created world. The goal of His purpose is not a collection of individual spirits abstracted one by one from their involvement in the world of matter and in the human community and set in a new and purely spiritual relation to Himself. Such a thought is irreconcilable with the biblical view of God, of man, and of the world. The redemption with which He is concerned is both social and cosmic, and therefore the way of its working involves at every point the re-creation of true human relationships and of true relationship between man and the rest of the created order. Its centre is necessarily a deed wrought out at an actual point in history and at a particular place. Its manner of communication is through a human community wherein men are re-born into a new relation one with another, and become in turn the means of bringing others into that new relationship; and through sacramental signs wherein man is restored to a true use of, and valuation of, the created world. Its law of working is not the direct approach of God to every man in the solitude of his own soul, an approach which would leave man still alone and therefore still unhealed, but the mediated approach through the neighbour and through the created world, an approach which in the very act of his response binds him to the neighbour and relates him truly to the created world. The means which God employs for our salvation are congruous at every step both with the nature wherewith He endowed us, when He created us and the world of which we are a part, and with the end to which He leads us, which is that all things should be summed up in Christ.

It is, I am sure, in the context of this biblical conception of the nature and scope of salvation that we are to understand that doctrine which is so basic to the biblical doctrine of the Church and yet capable of such terribly unbiblical distortion—the doctrine of election. If one starts, as so much Indian thought for instance does, from a conception of man and of the world in which the real is the spiritual, and all the rest is illusion, and in which salvation is conceived of as ultimately a matter of the relationship between each individual soul and God, then the whole idea of divine election appears as a piece of arbitrary favouritism, typical of an irresponsible potentate but unworthy of the God and Father of our Lord Jesus Christ. But once it is understood that salvation is corporate and cosmic, and that therefore the means which God employs for our salvation must be congruous with that end, it becomes clear that God must deal with us according to the principle of election. One race is chosen in order that through it God's salvation may be mediated to others, and it may thus become the nucleus of a new redeemed humanity. The apostles are chosen that they may go and bear fruit. Those to whom they bring the good news of salvation in Christ will be knit with them into the apostolic fellowship. It is true that at every step of the process there is an element of ultimate mystery which the mind of man cannot fathom. No one can say why it is that one was chosen and another not, why it is that here the word came 'not in word

THE COMMUNITY OF THE HOLY SPIRIT

only, but also in power, and in the Holy Ghost' (I Thess. 1. 5), while there the same word carried no regenerating power. The answer to that question is known only to God. But if we cannot know for what *reason* one was chosen, we can most certainly know for what *purpose* he was chosen: he was chosen in order to be a fruit-bearing branch of the one true vine (John 15.16), a witness through whom others might be saved. He is chosen in order that through him God's saving purpose may reach to others, and they too be reconciled to God in and through His reconciled and reconciling people. And while the ultimate mystery of election remains, one can see that the principle of election is the only principle congruous with the nature of God's redemptive purpose. And we can also see that wherever the missionary character of the doctrine of election is forgotten; wherever it is forgotten that we are chosen in order to be sent; wherever the minds of believers are concerned more to probe backwards from their election into the reasons for it in the secret counsel of God than to press forwards from their election to the purpose of it, which is that they should be Christ's ambassadors and witnesses to the ends of the earth; wherever men think that the purpose of election is their own salvation rather than the salvation of the world: then God's people have betrayed their trust. And wherever, on the other hand, the truth is grasped that God so loved *the world* that He gave His only begotten Son; that His purpose to redeem the world necessarily requires that men's salvation should be not by an unmediated act of God directed to each individual human soul in isolation, but by the operation of a love which works on the plane of human history, mediated by the concern of man for man knitting men into a visible community: then it is seen that this can only be by the way of election, by the choosing of one to be the channel of grace to his neighbour until all men are knit together in one redeemed fellowship.

It is clear that no discussion of the nature of the Church can avoid dealing with the doctrine of election, and it is also clear that this must come in the context of our discussion of the Church as the community of the Holy Spirit. Calvin in the *Institutes*, after treating of Christ's completed work of atonement by His death, resurrection and ascension, immediately goes on to say that it is by the secret working of the Holy Spirit that we enjoy Christ and all His blessings (III 1. 1), and then proceeds to a lengthy

Lincoln Christian College

exposition of regeneration as the work of the Holy Spirit, faith itself being treated primarily as one of the Spirit's fruits. This, surely, is the right and Scriptural order. It is by the work of the Holy Spirit alone that word and sacraments have power to mediate Christ to us, and that faith is given to us whereby to receive Him. And we are bound to go on to confess that this gift of the Holy Spirit is of God's pure grace, given to those whom He chooses according to the secret counsel of His will. It is all 'according to the election of grace' (Rom. 11. 5). This living presence and power of the Holy Spirit is the only source of our regeneration. All this we must surely confess. But we must also go on to insist that when this truth is taken in isolation out of its proper relation to the truth of the incarnation, the result has been a complete distortion of the Gospel. We know that this has in fact happened in the history of Calvinism. If instead of taking as the starting point of our thought the fact of Christ, we take the undoubted truth that God can choose and regenerate by the secret working of His Spirit whomsoever He will, it will inevitably follow that the actual work of Christ in history will come to take a place other than the determinative centre. The actual visible society which He founded will give place at the centre of our thought to the invisible number of the elect known only to God; the visible and tangible sacraments which He gave will seem less and less essential to salvation; the missionary task will be no longer integral to the very being of the Church, for—as the young William Carey was told—when God chooses to save the heathen He can do it without our aid; and—in the extreme development of this movement in Quakerism—even the Scriptures themselves will cease to have a central place, because the Spirit is directly given to every man and His witness requires no confirmation from any other source.

But the Gospel is good news of a very different kind. It is news of the actual fact that in Jesus of Nazareth, crucified in Palestine under Pontius Pilate, God was reconciling the world to Himself. It is He who is the elect of God, His beloved, His chosen One. Our election is only by our incorporation in Him. We are not elect as isolated individuals, but as members in His Body. The instrument of His choosing is precisely the apostolic mission of the Church. 'I chose you,' says the incarnate Lord to His apostles, 'and appointed you, that ye should go and bear fruit' (John 15.

16). At their first proclamation of God's saving acts these same apostles tell the multitude of their hearers: 'To you is the promise, and to your children, and to all that are afar off, even as many as the Lord our God shall call unto Him' (Acts 2. 39). And the great apostle of the Gentiles, recalling his first preaching to the Thessalonians, says to them: 'Knowing, brethren beloved of God, your election, how our gospel came not unto you in word only but also in power, and in the Holy Spirit, and in much assurance' (I Thess. 1. 4–5). The source of election is in the depths of God's gracious will 'before the foundation of the world'; its context is 'in Christ'; its instrument is the apostolic mission to the ends of the earth; its end is to sum up all things in Christ; and its means, seal and token is the presence of God's Holy Spirit—opening men's hearts to believe the Gospel, knitting them in love into the fellowship of the body of Christ, giving them in foretaste the powers of the age to come, and sealing them as Christ's until His coming again. The life of the visible Church on earth is thus the reality within which alone the doctrine of election is to be understood. The Church on earth is no mere earthly shadow of an invisible and heavenly substance. It is both the first-fruits and the instrument of God's gracious election, for His purpose is precisely the re-creation of the human race in Christ. In the same way the life of the visible Church is the reality within which alone the doctrine of the Holy Spirit is to be understood. We share in Christ's anointing only as we share in His body, in the baptism wherein we die with Him and are raised with Him, and in the common life wherein by the manifold gifts of the Spirit the body is built up in love and furnished with all that it needs for the prosecution of its divinely given mission.

IV

I want now to consider a further distortion which has in fact arisen from isolating the truth that the Church is the community of the Holy Spirit and treating this as alone determinative of its nature. It may be described, borrowing a phrase of Dr. John Mackay, as the setting of ardour against order. That problem had already appeared in the time of St. Paul, as his first letter to the Corinthians shows, and it has constantly reappeared. The preference for the abnormal and the spectacular, the belief that what is extempore and unprepared is more spiritual than what is customary or planned, the tendency to regard order and organisation as antithetical to the life of the Spirit—these are all evidences of a conception of the Holy Spirit more characteristic of the Old Testament than the New. In the Old Testament the Holy Spirit is spoken of mainly as a power coming upon individuals at particular times and enabling them to perform mighty works, to speak God's word, to discern His will. The New Testament begins by describing how the Holy Spirit descended upon Jesus and abode upon Him, and how in the power of the Spirit He lived and spoke, and how that same Spirit was given to His Church to be the permanent principle of its life. By this *koinonia*, common sharing, in the Holy Spirit, Christ's people are enabled to acknowledge Him as Lord, to cry to God as Father, and to live together a common life in which the Spirit furnishes all those gifts which such a common life needs and of which the greatest is love. The Holy Spirit is now no more an occasional visitant to a favoured individual, but the abiding and indwelling principle of life in a fellowship. The supreme gift of the Spirit is not the spectacular power by which an individual may gain pre-eminence, but the humble and self-effacing love by which the body is built up and knit together. It follows that a decisive mark of the Spirit's presence will be a tender concern for the unity of the body, a horror of all that exalts some human leader or some party into the place which Christ alone can occupy. We see that recoil of horror in St. Paul when he hears of the factions in the Church at Corinth. 'Is Christ divided? was Paul crucified for you? or were ye baptised into the name of Paul?', and a little later, 'Whereas there is among you jealousy and strife, are ye not carnal and walk after the manner of men?' (I Cor. 1. 13; 3. 3). All these blunt questions are intimately related to each other and together go far to illuminate the apostle's understanding of the Spirit. Life in the Spirit is life in the body of Christ, and factions in the Church involve the enormity of dismembering the body of Christ. Its basis is Christ's death once for all, which was indeed His baptism wherein all the world was baptised into His death, and by which it was made possible for us to be baptised into His death and so—dead to self—made sharers in His life. Henceforth He is our life, and therefore His is the only name by which we can call ourselves. To put the name of any man into that place, to call ourselves by the name of some man or some party, is to be carnal not spiritual. Life in the Spirit is precisely life in the one body of Christ, wherein there is no room at the centre for 'I' or 'we', but He is all in all. In the building up of the common life of the body there will be need for the due operation of the principles both of order and of freedom. Where these clash with one another there will be room for honest difference of opinion, and there will be need for a common seeking of the Spirit's guidance. But the mark of the man in Christ will be that he is more eager to claim freedom for his brother than for himself, and more ready to submit himself to good order than to impose it on his brother. In any case the fundamental principle will always be the love which seeks not its own good but the common good of the body. When the claim to possession by the Spirit, attested perhaps by abnormal signs of spiritual power, is made the ground for treating the unity and order of the Church with contempt, and for despising the great mass of 'nominal Christians' in whom only the virtues which we have come to regard as normal for a Christian are to be seen, we must say bluntly as St. Paul did, that this is not the work of the Spirit but of the flesh. There is one Body as there is one Spirit, and there are no grounds for thinking that we can try to separate one from the other without disastrous error.

I think that there are many whose churchmanship is of what I have loosely called the Pentecostal type, who would here hotly deny that they are indifferent to the unity and order of the Church. They would point to the very deep experience of fellowship which exists in their congregations, often so very much deeper than that of Churches which make much of the words 'order' and 'unity', and they would ask: 'What more than this are you asking for? Are you asking that we should all belong to some all-embracing organisation on a national or world-wide scale to which every congregation would be subject? Is that what you mean by order and unity? For if so, we must reply that we do not desire such an organisation, we do not find it in Scripture, and we do not believe it to be the will of God. We are persuaded that the Church in the New Testament is either the local congregation of believers, or else it is the whole company of believers in earth and heaven. We find no justification for any other use of the term.'

While I shall show reasons for disagreement with this protest, it contains elements of truth both in what it affirms and in what it denies. Positively, I think it is true that we must regard the local congregation as having a certain real primacy among the various units into which we may think of the Church as being divided. That body of neighbours who share in the same loaf and the same cup, who form the visible company in which the word is preached, and who, being neighbours, are able in the context of actual personal meeting to build one another up in the faith and to correct one another in love and to wait together on the Lord for His guidance, has a strong claim to be regarded as the primary unit of Christian fellowship. I venture to say that there is certainly very much more to be said for this claim than for the claim that the diocese, as commonly understood in the Anglican Communion today,[1] is the basic and indivisible unit of the Church's life. I think we must say that a real congregational life, wherein each member has his opportunity to contribute to the life of the whole body those gifts with which the Spirit endows him, is as much part of the *esse* of the Church as are ministry and sacraments. (In this connection I think it is significant that the 'Lambeth Quadrilateral', which has dominated all discussions on Christian reunion at least in Anglo-Saxon countries for the last thirty years, contains no reference to congregational life, fellowship and discipline.) Negatively I think our protesting friend is right in being afraid of certain kinds of supra-congregational organisation which have the effect of distorting the real character of the Church's life. The strong drift of our time is towards large-scale organisation with its attendant evils of mechanisation and bureaucracy, and the Churches have not been exempt from these. There is a real danger that the type of organisation proper to a large-scale modern political and cultural organisation would be imposed upon, and thereby distort, the quite different kind of life which is proper to the Church and which is most clearly seen in the life of worship, witness, mutual love and service, and prayer, of a Christian congregation. It is certainly true that the New Testament gives us no warrant for imposing such an organisation upon the life of the local church. I think that there is no doubt that one of the things which make

[1] Which is, of course, a different thing from a diocese in the primitive Church.

good Christian men suspicious of the movement towards re-union, is the belief that reunion means the creation of larger units of ecclesiastical administration. It is therefore most important to insist that it does not mean anything of the kind. Indeed, I think that in many cases it ought to lead to a drastic process of decentralisation and the development of smaller and more compact ecclesiastical units. Reunion has in itself nothing to do with the size of ecclesiastical units. It has to do with the recovery of the true nature and quality of the Church's life as the visible fellowship of all who in every place call upon the name of the Lord Jesus. But when all this has been admitted, as it must gladly be admitted, we must continue to press such questions as the following: Why should the local congregation be singled out as the only form of Christian collectivity to which all the qualities of the Church may be ascribed? If it be Christ's purpose to draw *all* men unto Himself, must not that purpose find some visible expression? May we not therefore expect, and do we not therefore find, that this gracious activity is expressed not only in the unity of a local congregation, but also on the one hand in the Christian family, and on the other in the Christian nation and in the ecumenical fellowship of Christians? If in our other human relationships we have to deal with men not only in our immediate neighbourhood, but also in other places and other countries, and are indeed bound to enter into all kinds of binding relations with them in the course of our political and economic life, how can it be that all these relationships beyond what is purely local should be outside of the sphere of redemption, and that in Christ we should have covenant relations only with our immediate neighbours? If in the experience of a local Christian fellowship we have known that there is in Christ a freedom which is not lost but gained by the willingness of each both to contribute his insight to the common seeking for the Spirit's guidance, and also to defer to the corporate insight of the whole body as to what that guidance is, on what principle do we deny that the same process can operate and ought to operate over a wider sphere? Are we not bound to accept the principle that (to quote the International Congregational Council of 1949) 'wider synods and courts of the Church should have the same sort of authority as the church meeting', an authority which is—to quote the same statement—'ministerial, not legalistic, coercive, and magisterial'?[1] And do we not see precisely such an authority being exercised over the local congregation both by the apostle Paul, and by the Council of apostles and brethren gathered in Jerusalem? We may well agree that much ecclesiastical use of power has been utterly unspiritual, and that the Church as a whole greatly needs the testimony of those who have learned in experience what it is to live together in a truly Spirit-filled local fellowship. But we must insist that there is no intelligible reason why we should be asked to acknowledge the spiritual authority of the local fellowship over the individual but to deny the spiritual authority of the regional or ecumenical fellowship over the local. And when we see—as we do see—a multiplicity of bodies, each claiming to be a fellowship based upon the common sharing in the Holy Spirit, yet denying any binding obligations towards one another, and apparently without any sense of shame about such a situation, and sometimes even proud of it, must we not say bluntly: 'Brethren, you deceive yourselves. This fissiparation, this proliferation of mutually irresponsible sects, is not a work of the Spirit but of the flesh. In your emphasis upon the primacy of the Spirit, and upon the fact that the Church is intended to be a Spirit-filled fellowship in which the Spirit's gifts are known and enjoyed and used for the edification of the Church and for witness to the world, you are right. But you are wrong in severing the Spirit from the body, in forgetting that as there is one Spirit so there is one body, and that the first and most excellent fruit of the Spirit is the charity which beareth all things, believeth all things, hopeth all things, and is glad to suffer for His body's sake, which is the Church.'

This leads me in conclusion to make one very specific application of this general reasoning. The modern ecumenical movement has hitherto been, in the main, a meeting place of the Catholic and Protestant streams of Christian faith and life. What I have called the Pentecostal stream has been largely outside of it. I have already expressed the conviction that its contribution is needed if the ecumenical conversation is to bear its proper fruit. For the absence of that contribution (by no means a complete absence), the Churches which are in the ecumenical movement must take a share of the blame. They have been too unwilling to pay heed to the radical criticism of their life which they would

[1] *The Nature of the Church*, p. 184.

have had to face. They have often been content to live too much
on their past reputation, to be too much at home in the world.
But one must frankly say that a very heavy responsibility rests
on the other side. The decades which have witnessed the rise of
the ecumenical movement have witnessed also the rise of innu-
merable bodies which, claiming exclusive possession of the Holy
Spirit, have separated themselves from their fellow Christians.
The growth of real charity between the great confessions which
form the main body of Christians has been matched by the growth
of an increasingly malicious and violent campaign of abuse from
those movements on the flank. The propaganda of these organisations against the ecumenical movement is marked in many cases
by such a blatant self-righteousness, and such a total negation of
all charity, that one is tempted to despair of them altogether. But
we must not yield to this temptation, for within these same
movements we must recognise authentic marks of the Holy
Spirit's presence, and also a witness to truth which the traditional
Protestant and Catholic alike need to learn. We must acknowledge that we without them cannot be made perfect. We must
therefore assure our brethren of our willingness to learn from
them in the fellowship of the ecumenical movement, and we
must at the same time bear witness to them concerning the things
which the Holy Spirit has taught us. We must ask them to recognise the evident tokens of the Spirit's working in the experience
of the ecumenical movement, especially in the growth of charity
where it had been almost wholly lacking. We must tell them
that in order to enter into the ecumenical conversation with us it
is not necessary for them to abandon any of their distinctive
convictions, but only to recognise us as fellow Christians sharing
with them—even though we be in error—the same Spirit. We
must ask them to consider whether by denying all fellowship
with us, they do not sin against the Holy Spirit who is in them,
and whether faithfulness to their Lord and ours does not absolutely require us to seek unity with one another.

And at the same time *we* must be willing to learn. In recent
discussions of the Catholic-Protestant issue, and of the deadlock
in which these discussions seem to have become immobilised, it
is often suggested that the way forward may be found in a new
understanding of the doctrine of the Holy Spirit. But of course
the illumination which is needed will never come as a result of

purely academic theological study. May it not be that the great Churches of the Catholic and Protestant traditions will have to be humble enough to receive it in fellowship with their brethren in the various groups of the Pentecostal type with whom at present they have scarcely any Christian fellowship at all? The gulf which at present divides these groups from the ecumenical movement is the symptom of a real defect on both sides, and perhaps a resolute effort to bridge it is the next condition for further advance.

V

CHRIST IN YOU, THE HOPE OF GLORY

WE began these lectures with the question: 'How are we made incorporate in Christ?' and we have considered the three types of answer which we have characterised as Protestant, Catholic and Pentecostal. I hope to have shown that all of these three are rooted in the very nature of the Gospel itself, and that the denial of any of them leads to the disfigurement of the Church and the distortion of its message. But this brings us face to face with the practical problem which so perplexes us. We are members of bodies separated from one another, each claiming to be the Church. The ground of this separation is the duty of bearing faithful witness to some part of this threefold truth which, it is felt, is compromised by others. Each body is compelled to regard what it holds as of the *esse* of the Church. Yet no body can admit that what others hold apart from it, is of the *esse* of the Church, for that would destroy its own claim to be the Church. We are drawn to one another by a real working of the Holy Spirit which we dare not resist, but we are prevented from accepting one another as Churches by loyalty to the very truth upon which our existence as Churches seems to stand. It is my purpose in the present lecture to seek to show that our incorporation in Christ has a dimension of eschatological depth which is incompatible with this whole way of looking at the Church, and which compels us to say that the Church can never be defined in terms of what it now is, but only in terms of the mercy of God 'who quickeneth the dead, and calleth the things that are not, as though they were' (Rom. 4. 17). Bearing in mind all that has been said about the threefold answer to our question, we have now to go forward and seek to penetrate so far as we may into the central mystery, our union in and with our crucified, risen, and ascended Lord.

I

I do not need to do more than remind you at the outset of the wealth of imagery with which the Scripture speaks of this union. We are members of Christ. We are the body of which He is the head. We are the branches and He the vine. He is the bridegroom and we the bride. We are spiritually joined to the Lord in a unity of one Spirit as close as the unity in which man and woman become one flesh. We are a temple and He the chief corner stone. We are a family and He is the elder brother. We are a new human race and He is the new Adam. We are the hungry pilgrims and He is the heavenly food giving eternal life. We are 'partakers of Christ', and He is, in fact, our life. The abundance and variety of the language reminds us both that this theme of our union with Christ belongs to the very heart of the New Testament message, and also that none of these phrases, taken alone and pressed to all its logical issues, can give us a true doctrine of it. We are dealing here with a reality which cannot be compassed in any single human figure of speech. So far, I take it, all will agree.

If we now press on to ask what is the central and determining mark of this union, I do not think there can be any doubt about the answer: it is union with His death and resurrection. Fr. Mascall in his very valuable book, *Christ, the Christian and the Church*, asks whether the re-creation of human nature is to be located in the union of human nature with the Person of the Word in the womb of Mary the Virgin, or in the death of the Lord Jesus on the Cross. He answers that both are necessary, though his own exposition is almost entirely centred on the first. We must agree with him that any attempt to set these two things over against one another is to be deplored, but surely there is some significance in the fact that the attention of the New Testament is overwhelmingly concentrated upon the second. When Fr. Mascall asks: 'Is it Lady Day or Good Friday that is the supreme commemoration of our redemption?', I should have thought the question answered itself. It surely does mean something that baptism is, by the universal consent of all Christians from the New Testament until today, baptism not into Christ's incarnation but into His death and resurrection. It means at least this, that at the heart of all that we rightly mean by our life in Christ and Christ's life in us, there is the fact of death. Let us not use here the word 'paradox', for it suggests something merely in the realm of thought. We are here dealing with no mere paradox for thought but with that actual death on Golgotha under Pontius Pilate, with that actual death of the old man in us without which none of us can put on the new man, and—let me add—with that actual dissolution of all things which must be before God's new heavens and new earth and all the glory of His kingdom can be revealed. We are dealing with all that is comprehended in the one central Christian sign—the sign of the Cross.

(i) We shall look first at those once-for-all events on which our redemption rests, and then at their reproduction in the life of the believing Church. We begin with the baldest reminder of the facts that Jesus, who was the Word of God incarnate, was rejected by men, condemned by the authorised teachers of the divine law, betrayed by one of His own chosen apostles, deserted by the rest, condemned by the anointed High Priest of God's Israel, and executed as a common criminal by the Gentiles. We go on to remember that all this is foreseen and interpreted by Him as that which *must* be, as that through which His mission is to be fulfilled, as that through which all men are to be drawn to Him. The victory of God's coming age can only be by what in this age is called defeat. The movement of redemption which begins with the breaking of the new age into this age at the incarnation does not thereafter take the form of a continuous movement through this world's history. There is no extension of the incarnation. Jesus who has come forth from the Father must return to the Father. It is necessary for him to go away, even though His going will mean also that all His own sheep will be scattered abroad (Mark 14. 27 and John 16. 32), for only so can the true continuation of His work begin (John 16. 13–14 and 20. 21–3). The new age and the present age, the reign of God and the reign of the prince of this world, cannot openly confront one another without one destroying the other. By His taking of human nature upon Himself and living a human life in this world, Christ has exposed Himself to all the powers of this dark world and they have combined to destroy Him. But by this deed He has taken upon Himself the whole curse of sin, manifested the righteousness of God, and broken the grip of Satan upon us. Yet this victory must remain hidden, for only so is there room left for the free response of faith, hope, and love. The full revelation of God's kingdom must mean the obliteration of all that is opposed to it, and God

H

in His mercy witholds that final revelation so that man may repent and believe. Until that day of Christ's coming in glory, His reign is to be known not by sight but by faith, not in full enjoyment but in foretaste, not in complete manifestation but in signs which point beyond themselves to a reality greater than themselves; and such signs were present in the ministry of the incarnate Lord, and in the ministry of the apostles as it is recorded in the Acts and Epistles (e.g. Acts 2. 43; 5. 12; 14. 3; 19. 11; Rom. 15. 19; II Cor. 12. 12, etc.). The supreme sign on which all else depends is the resurrection of Jesus from the tomb on the first Easter morning. This is the divine event without which the Church could not have been born. Had the tomb not been empty on that morning there would have been no Church. But it is at the same time a sign pointing beyond itself, a foretaste, the first fruits of a harvest yet to come (e.g. I Cor. 15. 20; Acts 26. 23; Rom. 8. 11). It is the place at which we are begotten again to a living hope for an inheritance yet to be revealed (I Pet. 1. 3). Without that sign the apostles could not have believed. And yet just as our own Lord rebuked those Jews who in the days of His flesh cared more for the signs than for the King whose reign the signs revealed, so He gently rebuked Thomas with the words, 'Because thou hast seen me, thou hast believed: blessed are they that have not seen, and yet have believed' (John 20. 29). The purpose of a sign is to point beyond itself; of a foretaste to make us long ardently for that which is yet to come. When, therefore, the Lord had gathered again His scattered flock and given them the assurance of His victory, He withdrew His visible presence from them at the ascension, assuring them again of His coming again, laying upon them the responsibility to fill the time that should be given to them with the task of summoning all nations to repentance and faith, and promising His presence with them to the end even though He was absent from sight and hearing and touch. They were to go forth proclaiming a victory which was real and yet still to be unveiled; hidden and yet manifesting its presence by signs which faith would recognise and grasp. That verse from the 110th Psalm which seems to have been often on their lips, as it was indeed used by the Lord Himself, perfectly describes this double character of His rule: 'The Lord said unto my Lord, Sit thou on my right hand, till I make thine enemies the footstool of thy feet.' He reigns, and yet His victory is still to be consummated. His reign is hidden, yet because He is at the right hand of the Father He grants signs of his kingship which faith will recognise and lay hold of. Such must necessarily be the mysterious, paradoxical character of Christ's presence in the midst of this world.

(ii) We meet this same mysterious and paradoxical character when we go on to consider the work of the Holy Spirit by whom Christ's saving deeds and words are taken and applied to us and by whom we are made members in Him. The account of these saving deeds which we have just given ended with the ascension. The counterpart of this withdrawal of Christ from the reach of the senses was the gift to the apostles of the Holy Spirit by whom Christ was made present to them in a new way. They now knew Him no more by sight and after the flesh: they had His Spirit. And this 'having' is both a real possession and a foretaste, an earnest of what is in store. It is a real supernatural infusion of the divine power by which they are enabled to know and do what is otherwise impossible. But at the same time the gift of the Spirit is a foretaste pointing onwards to the final victory. The Spirit assures us that we are heirs of a kingdom yet to be revealed (Rom. 8. 17). The Spirit wars in us against the flesh (Gal. 5. 17) and gives us the assurance that even our mortal bodies shall be quickened (Rom. 8. 11), and that what is mortal is to be swallowed up of life (II. Cor. 5. 4–5). Meanwhile the very mark of the Spirit's presence is that we groan waiting for our adoption (Rom. 8. 23) and hoping for that which we do not yet see (24–5). But yet this hoping is so grounded in what God has actually done (I Pet. 1. 3) and in the experience of the power of the Holy Spirit now, that we rejoice in it (Rom. 5. 2). This hope never puts us to shame, because the love of God has been shed abroad in our hearts through the Holy Spirit given to us (Rom. 5. 5). We are of Christ's household if we hold fast our boldness and the glorying of our hope firm to the end (Heb. 3. 6). This list of quotations might be extended almost indefinitely, to remind you that everything said in the New Testament about the life in Christ after the Spirit is shot through with this double quality. We died and our life is hid with Christ, yet we have to mortify our members and seek the things above. We are risen with Him, yet await the resurrection. We cry, 'Abba, Father,' yet wait for our adoption. The Church is Christ's bride—yet she longs for the marriage feast. He is with us always—yet we cry, 'Come, Lord Jesus.' Such must necessarily be the character of the life of the age to come in the midst of the life of this age—of the Church in the world. It is what it is not yet, it longs to be what it is.

Recent theological writing has made us very familiar with this paradox. But I have the feeling that we often state it in a way which looks more like some sort of conjuring trick with time and eternity than like something vital to our salvation. We must try to state the thing in a more religiously significant way if we are to make the point clear. In order to do so we must first look at a very closely related paradox which is expressed in a variety of ways in the New Testament, but which we can conveniently introduce by referring to St. Paul's intensely simple and personal statement to the Galatians: 'I have been crucified with Christ; yet I live; and yet no longer I, but Christ liveth in me: and that life which I now live in the flesh I live in faith, the faith which is in the Son of God, who loved me, and gave himself up for me' (Gal. 2. 20).

'I have been crucified with Christ.' The Christian life is first of all a dying, of which the source is the dying of the Son of God, One for all, and once for all. 'The love of Christ constraineth us: because we thus judge, that one died for all, therefore all died' (II Cor. 5. 14). Our dying with Christ is not a metaphysical abstraction. It is, if one may put it so, the soul's Amen to that final judgment upon the life of this world which was pronounced at the Cross, the judgment of holy love, of love suffering vicariously the curse of sin. Before the Cross where all man's wisdom and piety combined to crucify the Son of God, all mankind is found guilty of treason against the love of God. The first commentary on the crucifixion of Jesus is the suicide of Judas, who —when he saw what he had done—went out and hanged himself. The Cross is the end of all human wisdom, of all human righteousness, of all human power. Every man there stands condemned an enemy of God.

'Yet I live.'[1] I live because He died that I might live. His death

---

[1] I have followed here the Revised Version text, rather than the margin, which reads: 'and it is no longer I that live, but Christ', etc. If the marginal reading were preferred, the form of what I have written would have to be changed, but its substance would be unaffected. The statement 'I live' is implied by the latter part of the passage, and is in line with the other passages in St. Paul on the same subject (e.g. Col. 3. 3; II Cor. 5. 14-15; Rom. 6. 5-11).

was no empty gesture, no mere demonstration of goodwill from the far side of the chasm which sin opens between man and God. It was the mighty creative act of Him by whom all things were made, and its purpose towards me was that I might have life. The sentence of death which I bear in my own soul as I stand before the Cross is at the same time God's creative word by which new life is born, a new life which is not of the will of the flesh but of God. He loved me and gave Himself up for me. This worthless traitor soul was counted of more value than His own, and so He put Himself in my place and me in His; crossed the unbridgeable chasm and stood on my side and in my place as a sinner, that I might stand in His place as a child of God. I live because He, the Lord of life, gave His life for me: how, then, can I not live?

'Yet not I, but Christ liveth in me.' I live because He died for me, but yet this is not a mere reprieve for the old life. That life is dead and buried. It is rather a new life, a new sort of self-hood whose centre is in Him. He is its driving and directing power as He is its only source. It is His life in me replacing the old life that was crucified with Him. He, the risen Lord, is alive in me, I am a member of His body, I am a sharer in His risen life.

'The life which I now live in the flesh I live in faith, the faith which is in the Son of God, who loved me, and gave Himself up for me.' It is Christ's life in me, but yet it is also my life. I still live in the flesh. I am still an ordinary human being. But I live *in faith*—faith in Him. That means that I am always looking to Him, trusting Him, depending on Him, and hoping eagerly for the day when I shall see Him in all His splendour. If I lose this attitude of faith, of eager expectancy, of always 'looking to Jesus', and begin to think of my Christian life as a thing of my own, I have fallen from grace and begin to live not only 'in the flesh' but 'after the flesh'. Christ is, so to say, both the subject of the Christian life and also its object. I must say, 'It is no longer I that live, but Christ lives in me,' and at the same time say, 'I live in the flesh by faith in Christ.'

It is impossible to reduce this profound statement of the apostle to anything more straightforward. I am crucified yet I live. Yet not I but Christ. Christ lives in me, yet I live by faith in Christ. It is shot through and through with paradox. Yet every Christian has at least some experimental knowledge of its meaning when-

ever he stands before the Cross of Christ. The life in Christ, or
the life of Christ in us, can never be truly described in terms less
paradoxical than the apostle here uses.

The words which we have been studying are written from the
point of view of the individual believer. But of course the individual believer is not a mere individual. Every Christian has his life
in Christ only as a member in the body of Christ. He shares in
the life of Christ only by sharing it with all His people. The new
birth, the new man in Christ, is a social reality. The ego which
is crucified with Christ is the independent, self-sufficient ego. The
life of Christ in the believer is a corporate life in which he can
only share by sharing it with all. And equally the corporate life
of the Church is no other than this profoundly mysterious life
of Christ in us, which is to be described only in terms of paradox
—as a dying and yet living, as not we but Christ, and yet as our
life lived by faith in Christ; as a life lived under the double sign
of Cross and Resurrection, of death and life, and in the tension of
having and yet not having.

II

It will have been noticed that in trying to remind you of this
double character of the Church's life I have used without much
discrimination a number of different pairs of terms. It is now
necessary to distinguish them more carefully in order to show
how they are related to one another. I have spoken of the paradox
of life through death, of the paradox of 'having and yet not yet
having', and of the paradox 'I live, yet not I but Christ', which is
alternatively expressed by saying 'Christ lives in me, but I live
by faith in Christ.' These three are not all of the same kind or
on the same level of significance, but they are all related to one
another, and we must look at each of them separately.

1. *Life through death*. This is the basic fact upon which all else
rests. The revelation of God's power and righteousness and love
in this world of sin could only be under the form of weakness
and death. The powers of this age when confronted with the
manifestation of God's coming age, could only condemn and
destroy and thereby they brought upon themselves condemnation. Christ's resurrection is the sign that they are defeated, and
the time now given to us is a time in which we and all men

may accept the sentence of condemnation, put off the life of this age, and put on the new life which Christ has won for us, which He has in Himself and which He imparts to us. In this age, during which Christ is imperceptible to our senses, we are given through the Holy Spirit a real participation in His risen life through participation in His death. So far we are dealing not with a paradox for thought but with the actual facts of Christ's death and resurrection, and with the corresponding fact that it is only by the death of our sinful selves that we can be made partakers in Christ's risen life. The acute difficulty for thought arises from the fact that we both die and yet do not die. Everyone who has honestly faced the Cross of Christ knows what is meant by this dying with Christ and knows that it is a reality, a deep and costly reality. And yet he knows also that the self which has died is still alive and has to be continually fought to the death. He knows that the new life in Christ which he has received is something which has to be daily put on again. He knows that he has the new life only by faith, and that faith is a daily renewed fight against unbelief. It is this paradox of having, and yet not yet having, the new life in Christ which is the source of our deepest perplexities.

2. *Having and not yet having.* We have spoken of the fact that what seems at first sight to be a paradox—the paradox of life through death—is really our apprehension of the fact that God's reign could only be revealed in this world of sin under the form of defeat and death. The Bible speaks of this revealing of God's reign in terms of the breaking in of the age to come with all its powers into this present age. The pouring out of the Holy Spirit first upon Jesus and then upon the disciples, the miracles and signs which accompany their preaching as they accompanied His, and above all the resurrection itself, are evidences of the breaking in of 'the powers of the age to come' into 'this present age'. And yet, on the other hand, this present age has not ended: it is still, precisely, the present age. And though the powers of the age to come really are at work, it is still, precisely, the age to come! So that the two ages, so to speak, overlap, lie alongside one another, and fight with one another in the world and in the soul of every Christian.

What I am now saying has become a commonplace of theological discussion. It is certainly thoroughly biblical. But I continually find myself asking: 'What does it really mean?' When

one gets into the mood for it one can play around with the terms
'time' and 'eternity', and picture ages as though they were slabs
of extended stuff overlapping one another. But what does it really
mean to speak of the age to come being now at work in the
present? We cannot here avoid saying something about the
Christian understanding of time which is, in any case, so vital to
a true doctrine of the Church. For if we speak of the future being
already present, what is to prevent us from concluding that time
is really illusory, and that hope is therefore no vital part of the
Christian life? We are familiar with the profound difference
between Greek or Hindu conceptions of time which are cyclical
and therefore ultimately deny the possibility of a purpose in
universal history, and the biblical conception of time as linear.
But if in the Bible the future has broken into the present we have
to admit that the line has at least become badly kinked. Many
Christian scholars do, in fact, attempt to interpret the concept
of eternal life, or the life of the age to come, as a life which is
non-temporal and therefore—so to say—equidistant from any
point in time. Thus Fr. Mascall defines eternity as 'a mode of life
above and independent of time'. 'Eternity,' he says, 'is the mode
of life proper to God as time is the mode of life proper to us,'
and after speaking of 'eternal life' in the Johannine sense as a
communication to us here and now as creatures of a real participation in the divine eternity, he goes on: 'It is true that there are
other New Testament passages in which *zoe aionios* is spoken of
as something in the future which we have not yet attained; but
this only helps to bring out the point which is precisely that the
gift which, considered in relation to the chronological sequence
of the natural order, is in the distant future is, when considered
from the standpoint of our elevation into the order of supernature
and grace, already in our possession.'[1] The use of the spatial
metaphor of 'elevation into the sphere of supernature' inevitably
suggests that 'eternal life' involves a sort of escape from the time
process, and that in so far as we are partakers of eternal life we
shall not require to take the time process quite so seriously as
those who know nothing else. The effect of this would be to
remove hope from the centre of the Christian life, in so far as
hope is an eager pressing forward to the consummation of God's
purpose in history, and to leave only hope as a longing for one's

[1] *Christ, the Christian and the Church*, pp. 99–100.

personal attainment of the beatific vision. In strong contrast to this, Prof. Cullmann[1] has shown that in the Bible eternity is really infinite time and not a different sort of existence from the point of view of which time is not successive but simultaneous, and that 'the age to come' is really—from God's point of view, if one may put it so—still to come, *after* the end of this present age. The difficulty with this view is to explain in what sense the powers of the age to come are already at work, and eternal life already a possession of the believer.

I believe that the clue to the resolution of these difficulties is a strictly theological one—that it has to do with our doctrine of God as personal. As beings created in the image of God we know time as real, yet we have a real transcendence over it. We are in time and cannot stay its course, but we can remember the past, plan for the future, and thus—in some measure—contract a span of time into the compass of a single thought. We can, in a real sense, grasp the past and the future now. But this power in us is only partial and derivative. It is only to be rightly understood as part of God's creation of man in His own image and His summons to man to be the agent of His purpose. For God's transcendence of time is not partial and derivative as man's is, but complete, because time is the form of His creation. Yet as His creation is real to God, so, we must surely believe, time is real to God, though His relation to it is necessarily different from man's. He is master of it, determining its times and seasons and foreseeing the end from the beginning. Yet surely he does not transcend it in such wise that its successiveness is seen by Him as simultaneity. It seems to me that we have one important clue to the real meaning of eternity in the biblical idea of the Sabbath, God's Sabbath rest when all His works are done.[2] Time is the form of God's working and eternity the form of His rest. Both are equally real. Neither is merely our illusion. And He does not rest until His work is done. 'My Father worketh hitherto, and I work,' said Jesus. In that sense eternity is still future, really future, and we long for it. There remaineth yet a Sabbath rest for the people of God. Yet, as the same passage reminds us, 'we, which have believed do enter into that rest . . . For he that is entered into his rest hath himself also rested from his works, as God did from his'

[1] *Christ and Time.*
[2] I owe this thought to Edwyn Bevan: *Symbolism and Belief.*

(Heb. 4. 3, 10). We must believe that in the depth of His infinite being God is already at rest, for He already grasps, so to say, the end. We know that a mature and integrated human person can combine a vast output of labour with a deep inner rest: indeed the one is the condition of the other. We see it supremely in our Lord Himself. Yet this is not the motionless rest of supra-temporal eternity in the light of which all time is illusion, the repose of the Vedantin who has reached the motionless centre of all things and can therefore leave the cosmic wheel to go on spinning endlessly and aimlessly round him. It is a rest which is held in tension with ceaseless labour, and the name of that tension is hope.

If we are right, then, in seeking a strictly theological interpretation of the relation of time and eternity, of seeing it as the relation between God's work and God's rest—and it seems to me that this is what the Bible indicates—this will give us the clue to the Christian experience of eternal life now, and it will be a Christological clue. Because Christ is God and Man, there is in Him both the power of the age to come and the enduring of the contradiction of sinners against Himself, both eternal life (the life of the age to come) and complete involvement in the life of the present age. And those who are in Christ, the Church which is the body of Christ, will be sharers in both. We can see now that this is no juggling with words. It is a matter of our personal relation with Christ. In so far as we are in real communion with Him, we share in Him, the Sabbath rest which remains for the people of God; and we share at the same time His suffering in the present age. We are given His Spirit, who is the very Spirit of God, and who reveals to us the deep things of God, in order that we may both know His peace and also be armed for His warfare. Above all, it is through the Spirit that we acquire that authentically Christian gift—the gift of hope, hope which never puts us to shame, 'because the love of God hath been shed abroad in our hearts through the Holy Spirit which was given unto us' (Rom. 5. 5). Hope in the Christian sense is no mere human longing for an uncertain future. It is rooted in the life of God Himself and founded on His own promises. It is the echo in our hearts, given to us by the Spirit, of that mind which was in Jesus who for the joy that was set before Him endured the Cross, despising the shame. It is an anchor of the soul, a hope sure and steadfast and entering into that which is within the veil. The future is really future, and we long for it. The whole creation groans with longing for it. Yet we do not *merely* long for it. We know that He has promised it and therefore we *hope*. And we know Him, and therefore we already share in some measure His perfect rest—the joy of journey's end.

It seems to me very important to state the paradox of having and not yet having in this way, because there is a danger that in simply speaking of time and eternity as two overlapping or simultaneous realities, we cut the nerve of hope. The age to come is still to come. We are to hope for it and to work for it. We cannot now enjoy it because God purposes something greater—a corporate and a cosmic salvation, and because it is His will to give time wherein men may repent and come to the free decision of faith, time therefore in which all men may have opportunity so to do. About this we have to speak more in the next lecture. The new age is still to come. Time is not an illusion. It is real and it is short. 'Now is salvation nearer to us than when we first believed' (Rom. 13. 11). Yet we do now enjoy a real foretaste of that salvation, a real foretaste of eternal life—real, yet a foretaste. And we enjoy it precisely in Christ, through our personal union with Him, for He has eternal life in Him, being God and Man. 'God gave unto us eternal life, and this life is in his Son' (I John 5. 11). Here the Pentecostal has surely been right as against both the orthodox Protestant and the Catholic; against the Protestant in expecting and welcoming wholeheartedly a real manifestation of the supernatural power of the Holy Spirit in the life of the believer in this present age; against the Catholic in recognising that this is only a foretaste which must never be allowed to blunt the keen edge of hope. Where he has been wrong is in failing to recognise that the supreme supernatural gift of the Spirit is love, and that therefore the proper counterpart of the one Spirit is the one body.

But this leads us directly to the third of our paradoxes—that which concerns our personal union with Christ—and to this we must now turn.

3. '*I live, yet not I; Christ lives in me.*' We have already noticed how the apostle, in seeking to convey in words what it means to be in Christ, is forced to use these paradoxical expressions. 'I am crucified. Yet I live. Yet not I but Christ. I live in the flesh in

faith—faith in the Son of God who loved me and gave himsel
up for me.' The fundamental fact is death in order to live. The
sinful, self-sufficient self must die to make room for Christ. But
what is the new life which follows? It is not my old life resusci-
tated. It is Christ's life in me. Yet we cannot simply say that and
leave it. *I* still live. Why is this? It is partly a matter of the paradox of having and yet not yet having, which we have already
discussed, the paradox of the overlap of the ages. But it is more
than this, for even in the age to come the *I* will not simply be
obliterated. Christ's life in me will still be also my life in Christ.
What is to be obliterated is the self which is centred in itself, in
order to make room for the self which is centred in Christ. This
is in truth self-hood proper to man as God willed him to be when
He created all things through Christ. But in fact man's self-hood
is so centred in himself that his re-creation into the true image,
into the last Adam, can be described from the point of view of
existing humanity only as death, just as it could be accomplished
only by the actual death of the last Adam under Pontius Pilate.
The re-created self-hood is true self-hood just because it is self-
hood centred in Christ. Man's true life as the image of God is
only 'in Christ', with the centre outside himself. From the point
of view of the self-centred self this can only be described in terms
of paradox: 'I am dead; yet I live: yet not I but Christ: I live in
the flesh.' But yet it is also possible to describe it in terms which
any Christian child can understand: 'I live by faith in the Son of
God who loved me and gave himself up for me.' This *is* true self-
hood—a life whose centre is Christ, a life in which the life of the
believer and the life of Christ mutually interpenetrate, of which
the very essence is a bond, a relationship constituted by His love
for me and accepted in my faith in Him issuing in an answering
love to Him and to all men. I have said that any Christian child
can understand what that means. Yet the Scripture teaches us to
find there the very heart of the Church's being. 'The glory which
thou hast given me I have given unto them; that they may be
one, even as we are one; I in them, and thou in me, that they may
be perfected into one; that the world may know that thou didst
send me, and lovedst them, even as thou lovedst me' (John 17.
22–23). The Church is called to be a union of men with Christ
in the love of the Father whereby their separate beings are made
one with that perfect mutual interpenetration in love, that perfect

community which is the glory of God. The final paradox of the Church's being is simply the paradox of which all know something who know what love is—the mutual losing of isolated self-hood to find it in the beloved. And, as we have seen, it is only within this understanding of our union with Christ in the mutual interpenetration of love that we can rightly understand what we have called the paradox of the eschatological overlap. It is only because we are in Him and He in us that we taste the powers of the age to come and have the foretaste of eternal life.

We still live 'in the flesh, in faith'. So long as we are in the flesh, it is by faith that we live. And faith is both a personal trust in Him whom we do not see, *and* the substance—the title-deed— of that for which we hope. The attempt to drive a wedge between faith in St. Paul and faith in Hebrews, between faith as a relationship of gratitude, trust and obedience towards the living Lord and faith as the anticipation, the title-deed, of the salvation to be revealed, is misguided. Faith is the second because it is the first. We have the foretaste of that which is to come only because we are united with Christ now. But the manner of our union with Him now in the flesh is not sight but faith. Our citizenship is in heaven, from whence we wait for a saviour. But precisely because He has withdrawn Himself from sight and gone to the Father, His Spirit has been given to us. We therefore possess Him in a way in which the disciples in the days of His flesh could not possess Him. He is in us and we in Him. We are made members of His Body. Yet again this possession is such that it can never be simply 'ours'. We possess Him only as we daily undergo that dying to self and that receiving of His risen life which is ministered to us by the Holy Spirit in the word and sacraments of the Gospel, and in the daily life of the fellowship which He rules. We are still in the flesh because His coming again awaits the fulfilment of His commission, because time must be given for all nations to believe, because we, without them, cannot be made perfect. Because we are still in the flesh, the flesh lusts against the rule of the Spirit. The lust of the old self for self-sufficiency still persists. We desire a greater security than this ever new, ever perilous dependence on the living Spirit, this daily dying. We shrink from facing that word which is the law of life for the Church no less than for the individual Christian: 'Whosoever would save his life shall lose it; and whosoever shall lose his life for my sake and the gospel's shall save it' (Mark 8. 35). We desire to see the Church as a body which *possesses* the grace of God, which is *in itself* the ark of salvation. Having received the heavenly riches we want to bury them in a napkin so that we know exactly where they can be got, rather than risk them in the constant traffic of the market place. Against all these very human and yet deadly perversions, the Spirit witnesses to us in word and sacrament that we are made Christ's only by being dead and buried with Him, that our baptism is baptism into His death, and our communion a communion in His broken body and shed blood, that our life—the life of the Church—is a hidden thing and must remain so, until the day when He appears again in glory. Equally the Spirit witnesses in word and sacrament to the fact that we do not *yet* possess the inheritance laid up for us, and that we are summoned at every stage to forget those things which are behind and to press on towards the goal which is still before us. We have in the sacrament of the supper a real participation in Christ: yet at every supper we are to remind ourselves that it is 'till He come'. Once this tension of longing and hope, this pressing forward to the goal which is still beyond our sight, goes out of the Christian life, we cease to be—in the apostolic sense—partakers of Christ (Heb. 3. 14). Our life in the flesh is to be a life of faith in Him, and faith is *both* a personal trust in Him who has loved us and given Himself for us, *and* the assurance of His coming again which, being already the substance of things hoped for, can endure as seeing Him who is invisible; and it is the second because it is the first.

III

The Church's life in Christ is thus a unique supernatural life which, from the point of view of our human language, must be described in paradoxical terms: a dying with Him in order to live with Him; a being in Him, yet hoping for His appearing; a life of which we must say both 'He lives in me' and 'I live by faith in Him.' I have sought to show how these three pairs of terms are related to one another, and how they all finally lead into the simple yet inexhaustibly profound statement that our life in Christ is a sharing in the love of God, the love which is the life of God, which unites the Father and the Son in the Spirit in that ultimate mystery of trinity in unity which is the source and the goal of all created being. Yet this sharing in the divine love is still as yet 'in the flesh in faith'. It is only maintained in an ever-renewed dying to self, and an ever-renewed pressing forward to the fullness of that which we have only in foretaste through the Spirit by faith. The true mark of the man in Christ will be that the more he grows in holiness the more will he know that he is a sinner, and the more will he long for and press on towards the fullness of sanctification 'with all the saints'. That paradox, familiar to every Christian, is perhaps the simplest way of expressing the paradox of the Church's being. The moment the Church begins to think that it possesses the fullness of divine grace, it has fallen from that grace. This means that Luther was surely right in saying that justification by faith is an article by which the Church stands or falls. The Church is both holy and sinful, because for man 'in the flesh' the only true holiness is that which renounces every claim to a righteousness of its own and casts itself only upon the grace of God in Jesus Christ.

But if this is true, then Luther abandoned his deepest insight when he substituted for the true, biblical picture of a Church both holy and sinful, a false and unbiblical distinction between the spiritual Church and the material Church or between the invisible Church and the visible Church. Both of these related pairs of terms have the effect of relaxing the true eschatological tension which is involved in recognising that in Christ we, along with all our brethren, are accepted as His while we are yet sinners, and of substituting an essentially legalistic and pharisaic conception that some are—so to say—in the Church by right and others only by grace. I know that this will be vehemently denied, but I think it is true. Even Calvin surely shows less than his usual clarity when he says that since we need some knowledge of who are to be regarded as the children of God, but do not need full certainty, God has, in place of certainty, 'substituted the judgment of charity by which we acknowledge all as members of the Church who by confession of faith, regularity of conduct, and participation in the sacraments, unite with us in acknowledging the same God and Christ' (Inst. IV, 1. 8). Surely we must ask whether this charity by which the hypocritical professor is admitted to be a member of the visible Church is, or is not, the same charity by which Calvin himself hopes to be saved on the Last Day. The holiness of God communicated to men in the body of Christ is

known in the flesh by faith as that which both saves and judges,
as that which we have and have not, as that by which we are
both accepted as God's children and yet condemned as sinners.
That is our situation in the flesh—*simul justus et peccator*—and we
are in it together. We long ardently for the day when we shall
be like Him, for we shall see Him as He is, though this longing
is not incompatible with a godly fear, lest, having preached to
others, we ourselves should be castaways. The final judgment
belongs to God alone on the last day. We are to judge nothing
before the time. Every attempt to slacken that eschatological tension by supposing now some sort of true Church within the
Church, involves a concealed—and sometimes open—pharisaism.
'Hypocritical professors' or—to use the modern term—'nominal
Christians' are always other people! When this attempt is allied
with a distinction between the so-called spiritual Church and the
so-called material or institutional Church, a distinction which
violates the whole biblical doctrine of the unity of creation, then
the way is opened wide for a profoundly unevangelical and un-
Catholic sectarianism.

In the light of this understanding of the paradoxical position
of the man in Christ we must criticise many of the debates which
have divided Christians from one another. It has been repeatedly
said in recent discussions of the nature of the Church that it is
vital to hold that being in Christ is an ontological fact involving a
change in the depths of our being, and not simply a new relationship with God. This is a development of the classical reformation
controversy as to whether righteousness was imputed or imparted.
These debates will be sterile so long as it is thought that man in
the depths of his being is something which can exist apart from
God, so long as it is not remembered that man's humanity exists
only in relation to God and is only truly human when it is in the
relation to God for which it was made. If there were a righteousness which man could have of his own, then we should have to
concern ourselves with the question how it can be imparted to
him. But there is not. The idea of a righteousness of one's own
is the quintessence of sin. Against this, therefore, against every
trace of a holiness or righteousness which does *not* depend simply
upon God's mercy to the sinner, we have to set our faces as relent-
lessly as Paul did. But equally with Paul we have to recognise
that if any man be in Christ there is a new creation, not a fiction

but a real supernatural new birth, the life of the risen Christ in the soul. From this life of Christ in us come forth the fruits of His presence—real and recognisable fruits, real holiness of life. But the manner of His indwelling is such as absolutely to preclude all thought of a holiness of one's own. The true analogy has been given by Him in His prayer to the Father: 'I in them, and thou in me, that they may be perfected into one.' The life of the Church is a real participation in the life of the triune God, wherein all life and all glory consist in self-giving, a *koinonia* wherein no one will ever say that aught of the things which he possesses is his own. The ultimate mystery of the Church's being is the mystery of love, and love 'seeketh not its own'. It is the very antithesis of its nature to calculate and divide between mine and thine. It will show its real presence in the redeemed best by ascribing everything to the redeemer.

Love must be the finally normative term in all thought about the Church, for love alone belongs to the last things which abide after all else is dissolved. It is true that we do not yet know much about love in its fullness. We see through a glass darkly. But we know that love is the supreme *arrabon*, the supreme foretaste of God's eternal life, the first and greatest gift of the Spirit. While we are in the flesh we must live by faith in Christ and hope for His appearing. We do not see Him but we trust Him utterly for what He has done and we believe His promise of what He will do. It is only by faith that we can receive the gift of His life in us, whereby love is born, and by unbelief we can lose it and be severed from Christ (Gal. 4. 19; 5. 4–5). But faith will be outdated when sight comes. Similarly we live by hope, rejoicing in that which we do not yet see, and hastening forward towards the prize of our high calling. But hope also will vanish into sight. That which abides is love—the same love which we now know in foretaste through the Spirit. Love is thus the concrete earnest of eternal life, and in it we have already experience of a relationship with Christ in which it is unthinkable that we should ascribe anything to ourselves of righteousness or holiness, in which we rejoice to acknowledge that He alone is our righteousness, our holiness, our life. If that be condemned as a merely psychological or relational statement and not an ontological one, we must surely answer that there is nothing deeper or more fundamental to man's being than this, that he was made in and for the love of God,

I

and that any attempt to seek an ontological core to his being apart from this is vain. 'He that abideth in love abideth in God, and God abideth in him' (I John 4. 16). There is no more profound way of describing the new man in Christ than that.

From within the experience of the love of God shed abroad in our hearts through the Holy Spirit we are enabled to see that the paradoxes in which we are bound to describe our incorporation in Christ are not ultimate self-contradictions but are the refraction of God's glory within the world which is passing away. Within the eternal being of God love is a never-ceasing self-emptying and out-pouring, forever met by the same out-poured love, the love of the Father and the Son in the unity of the Spirit. Eternal life is no motionless serenity, but love meeting love, the rapture of mutual love forever poured out and forever received. Herein lies the error of making an absolute and final distinction between *agape* and *eros*, for love in its perfection is both a giving and a receiving in which neither is calculated or delimited because both are complete. But within a world wherein love has become self-love, God's glory can be revealed only in the form of a Cross where the life-giving stream of divine love is poured out in utter self-giving in the waste-land of man's futile self-seeking. In the final consummation of God's loving purpose we and all creation will be caught up into the perfect rapture of that mutual love which is the life of God Himself. What is given to us now can only be a foretaste, for none of us can be made whole till we are made whole together. The very meaning of the word salvation is that it is a making whole, a healing of that which sunders us from God, from one another, and from the created world. The idea of a salvation that is a completed experience for each of us privately, apart from the consummation of all things, is a monstrous contradiction in terms. It belongs to the very character of the divine love in which, through Christ, we have been made participants, that we should for His sake be content to wait and to hope; to groan waiting for our adoption, the redemption of our bodies, and the revealing of the sons of God; and meanwhile to bear about in the body the dying of Jesus, that His life may be made manifest in us. The study of the paradoxes of the Christian life led us forward into the mysterious simplicity of love. We now see that love itself is that which sends us out to bear the pain of these paradoxes—of having and yet not having, of dying as the condition of life. For the love wherein we have been made participants cannot be satisfied until its work is done, the fullness of the nations gathered in and creation's lost harmony restored. Until that day, love itself bids us suffer without despairing and gives us patience to watch, to labour, and above all to pray for its coming.

IV

I began these lectures by asking: 'What is the manner of our incorporation in Christ?' I have tried to show that all the three answers which we looked at are true; we are made members in Him by hearing and believing the Gospel, by being received sacramentally into the visible fellowship of His people, and both of these only through the living presence of the Holy Spirit. At the same time I tried to show that when any one of them was taken as alone decisive, error and distortion followed. In the present lecture I have tried to show that our incorporation in Christ is to be understood in terms of the eschatological tension of faith and hope, both finding their ultimate meaning in love. By faith we accept Christ's dying and rising on our behalf, and ourselves become partakers in it; living still in the flesh, yet we are sharers in His life by faith. In hope we press forward to the full revelation of that victorious life of Christ which is now hidden. But while faith and hope are thus the marks of the new life in this age, its abiding inner reality is love—a love which is a sharing in the very life of the triune God. The love which is shed abroad in our hearts by the Holy Spirit, creating and sustaining faith and hope in us, is but the earnest of our full sharing in the love of God with all the saints—of our being perfected into one in the Father and the Son. But it is a *real* earnest. There is an actual sphere of redemption, of which the historical centre is Jesus Christ incarnate, crucified, risen and ascended. From that centre the word of salvation goes out to all the earth, the nations are baptised, the Lord's table is spread, a real community is built up—all by the living sovereign working of the Holy Spirit. It is here, in this visible community, that God is savingly at work reconciling the world to Himself, precisely because the salvation which He purposes is not merely private and spiritual but corporate and cosmic.

This being so, the very essence of the Church's life is that she is pressing forward to the fulfilment of God's purpose and the final revelation of His glory, pressing forward both to the ends of the earth and to the end of the world, rejoicing in the hope of the glory of God. The treasure entrusted to her is not for herself, but for the doing of the Lord's will, not for hoarding but for trading. Her life is to be forever spent, to be cast into the ground like a corn of wheat, in the ever-new faith and hope of the resurrection harvest. Her life is precisely life under the sign of the Cross, which means that she desires to possess no life, no security, no righteousness of her own, but to live solely by His grace. When she becomes settled, when she becomes so much at home in this world that she is no longer content to be forever striking her tents and moving forward, above all when she forgets that she lives simply by God's mercy and begins to think that she has some claim on God's grace which the rest of the world has not, when in other words she thinks of her election in terms of spiritual privilege rather than missionary responsibility, then she comes under His merciful judgment as Israel did.

In relation to our present argument I think this means that we must abandon the attempt to define the Church's *esse* in terms of something that it has and is. Behind the familiar distinction between *esse* and *bene esse* as used in arguments between Churches, there seems to lie—perhaps unconsciously—the idea that we can find some minimum of visible marks which will enable us to say: 'This is a Church and God must recognise it as such. More than this may be desirable but it is not essential. Less than this a body cannot have without forfeiting its participation in the Body of Christ.' If our argument has been sound, we must completely abandon this way of thinking. If man is made in the image of God, then man as we know him is a creature who has contradicted his own *esse*. He is maintained in existence only by the mercy of God and in order that he may be given time to repent and by faith to receive again the true image by his incorporation in the risen life of Jesus Christ. The Church's life in the flesh is within this total paradox of grace and is itself the clue to it. The Church does not exist by virtue of something which it is in itself. It exists only by the mercy of God 'who calleth the things that are not, as though they were' (Rom. 4. 17). Every attempt to define it by marks ascertainable by simple observation and apart from faith, violates the law of its being. The Church exists, and does not depend for its existence upon our definition of it. It exists wherever God in His sovereign freedom calls it into being by calling His own into the fellowship of His Son. And it exists solely by His mercy. God shuts up and will shut up every way except the way of faith which simply accepts His mercy as mercy. To that end He is free to break off unbelieving branches, to graft in wild slips, and to call 'No people' His people. And if, at the end, those who have preserved through all the centuries the visible 'marks' of the Church find themselves at the same board with some strange and uncouth late-comers on the ecclesiastical scene, may we not fancy that they will hear Him say—would it not be like Him to say—'It is my will to give unto this last even as unto thee'? Final judgment belongs to God, and we have to beware of judging before the time. I think that if we refuse fellowship in Christ to any body of men and women who accept Jesus as Lord and show the fruits of His Spirit in their corporate life, we do so at our peril. With what judgment we judge we shall be judged. It behoves us therefore to receive one another as Christ has received us.

I know that this is just what most of us are unwilling to do. We feel that other Churches must accept, as the *pre-condition* of fellowship, such changes as will bring them into conformity with ourselves in matters which we regard as essential, and that failure to insist on this will involve compromise in regard to what is essential to the Church's being. But for precisely the same reason we cannot admit a demand from others for changes in ourselves which would seem to imply a denial that we already possess the *esse* of the Church. And even a proposal to make these concessions mutual and simultaneous does not solve the difficulty. It may appear to 'save face', but at the cost of losing the integrity of faith.

All this way of thinking rests upon a static and non-temporal conception of the Church as something which possesses the fullness of its being here and now. If the argument of these lectures is true we have to abandon this altogether, and to conceive of the Church in the perspective of a real *eschaton* for which we wait in faith and hope, still involved in this sinful age and yet living by the mercy of God. This acceptance of a real end means that the dimension of time is a reality within the life of the Church, and that we must therefore ask of a Church not only 'What is it now?' but 'What is it becoming?' To accept one another as we are does not mean leaving one another as we are. It is precisely the beginning of a process of mutual correction and of speaking truth in love to one another in a way that is impossible so long as we do not treat one another as brethren. For if the Church exists only *by* His mercy, it exists *for* the doing of His will. He has given us sufficient knowledge of what His will is. It is that we should be His witnesses to the uttermost parts of the earth, preaching the Gospel, doing the mighty works of the Kingdom, baptising the nations, and bringing all men into the one fellowship whose visible centre is the sacrament in which we are partakers of His risen life and show forth His death till He come. There is no body of Christians which does not depart in some or all these respects from His will. We have too long devoted our strength to mutual accusation and to self-defence, on the basis of what the Churches *are*. Surely it is time for us to meet one another in penitent acknowledgment of our common failure to be what the Church ought to be. On the basis of what we are, none of us can be said to possess the *esse* of the Church. That is the real truth of our situation. There was a stage in the ecumenical debate at which the formula suggested for our mutual acceptance was: 'All have won, and all shall have the prizes.' Surely it is precisely the reverse of this that we must acknowledge. 'They have all turned aside, they are together become unprofitable.' The place of our meeting will not be the place where, in our easygoing way, we can decide—after all—to let bygones be bygones. It will be none other than the mercy-seat where alone Christ meets with us, the place where we know that we are sinners against God. Nothing that the Church *is* can provide us with our basis of assurance. Our only basis of assurance is the mercy of Christ who calls His Church to be His own glorious bride, without spot or wrinkle or any such thing. None of us has any standing save in that mercy. The mark of our calling will surely be a looking forward and a hurrying forward which are a sort of echo of the grace of God who quickens the dead and calls the things that are not as though they were, a determination to cease judging one another for what we are, and to build one another up in faith and hope and love into what He has called us to be.

VI

UNTO ALL THE NATIONS

I HAVE tried to show in the previous lecture that the Church can be rightly understood only in an eschatological perspective. Whenever we seek to define it simply in terms of what it is, we go astray. One might express the truth in a rather violently paradoxical way by saying that the Church is not what it is because it exists by the mercy of God who calls the things that are not as though they were. The Church is not merely a historical reality but also an eschatological one.

But we must now go on to say with the utmost possible emphasis that this statement carries with it immediate practical implications and if it is severed from these implications it becomes untrue. The meaning of this 'overlap of the ages' in which we live, the time between the coming of Christ and His coming again, is that it is the time given for the witness of the apostolic Church to the ends of the earth. The end of all things, which has been revealed in Christ, is—so to say—held back until witness has been borne to the whole world concerning the judgment and salvation revealed in Christ. The implication of a true eschatological perspective will be missionary obedience, and the eschatology which does not issue in such obedience is a false eschatology. It is too easy for us to use the biblical word 'world' as a mere abstract noun without really thinking of the concrete reality which the word denotes; to speak of the judgment of the world, the redemption of the world, the end of the world, without accepting the hard geographical meaning of the word. In this we depart altogether from the New Testament, where the names of actual countries and the details of actual journeys and the hopes and hazards of actual missionary adventure are all the time inextricably intertwined with theology. If, as theologians, we talk about the world, without meaning India, China, Africa, Russia, South America, as well as our own people, without meaning this actual globe and the nations which people it, we are talking unbiblical nonsense. Our doctrine of the Church will be distorted if it is not held in the perspective of a salvation which embraces the ends of the earth as well as the end of the age. It must be our first task in this concluding lecture to indicate the biblical evidence for these assertions.

I

1. In Christ the end of the world has been revealed. The day of the Lord has come. The kingdom of God has drawn near. But the powers of this age, not knowing the Lord of Glory when He came to His own, rejected and condemned Him. Thus the power and the wisdom of God were revealed in the weakness and foolishness of the Cross, His glory in its shame, His righteousness in its curse. The world thought that another false messiah had been brought to book, but, to those whom He had before designated as His witnesses, the real meaning of what had happened was disclosed in the fact of the Resurrection. This event, in the reality of which they only slowly came to believe, was seen to be the earnest, the first fruits of a universal and cosmic salvation, for in it death, decay, and corruption had been destroyed and Christ had been revealed as cosmic Lord. When this was grasped the obvious question was, 'Lord, dost thou at this time restore the kingdom to Israel?' (Acts 1. 6). If the kingdom has come, why is it not at once revealed in its full triumph? Why is the visible fulfilment of the ancient promises to Israel any further delayed? What do we wait for, and how long must we wait? How long do these last days last?

The answer to these questions (Acts 1. 7–8) is a warning and a promise and a commission, followed by the withdrawal of Christ's visible presence and the promise of His return. We must look at these things in their relation one to another in order to see their bearing on the nature of the Church's existence in this time between Christ's coming and His coming again.

2. In the first place there is a warning. The times and seasons are wholly in God's authority. The kingdom is wholly God's. The time and manner of its victory are wholly in His hands. He knows, and He alone, what are the limits of this world's history, when all its possibilities have been exhausted. The final consummation and victory are not simply the product of historical developments which we might in principle calculate. Nor are

they fixed by an arbitrary decree to whose secrets we might hope to have access. They are in the Father's hands. The decision is His, because the kingdom is His.

This means that we do not know what are the limits of human history, but it does not mean that there are no real limits. It is important to assert this, because if we do not do so, the limit which we know apart from Christ becomes determinative of our outlook. That limit is death—the death of the individual, and the death of the social structure in which his corporate personality is embodied. When these are the only limits that men know, then they are left in a hopeless alternation between hope for an individual survival of death, which evacuates their corporate life of ultimate significance, and hope for the eternity of some social or political or cultural achievement, which evacuates personal existence of ultimate significance. This false alternation is overcome in Christ in whom we are brought into relation with the true limit—a consummation of all things in which both the significance of each personal life and the significance of history as a whole are to be gathered up. In Him death has been overcome and is therefore seen to be no longer the absolute limit of history. In Him we are brought face to face with the true end. Yet because in Him the end is revealed but not yet consummated, we still remain within the limit of death, living still in the flesh by faith, and knowing that we must die. Yet we both live and die in hope—hope for an event as certain as death, though, like death, an event whose time we do not know. That event is the coming again of Christ to consummate His victory and to reign for ever. The day and the hour we know not. That He shall come again we know. His coming in the flesh is the revelation of the end of history, yet in such wise that space is given for belief and unbelief. His coming again will be the end itself, wherein faith will at last be taken up into sight and hope into fruition. The time that is given is finite, because the victory that we hope for is real. Now is salvation nearer to us than when we first believed—salvation, the final making whole of all things in Christ. The time is finite and therefore precious. It is given precisely that all men may have the opportunity to repent and believe, to awake out of sleep, cast off the works of darkness, and put on the armour of light. Only the Father can know the day when the harvest is ripe and all things are ready to be gathered up. He waits for that day, waits for our obedience. The warning that it is *not* given to us to know the times or the seasons leads to the statement of what *is* given —the commission to be His witnesses to the ends of the earth.

3. But first there is given the assurance of the Spirit's power, granted for the task of witness. 'Ye shall receive power, when the Holy Spirit is come upon you: and ye shall be my witnesses.' Although the final victory is not yet revealed, the gift of the Spirit is the sign of its coming, for our sharing in Him is a foretaste of the powers of the age to come. The Spirit is given us in order that we may be witnesses, for He is the primary witness to Christ, bringing the world now under the judgment which is the final judgment, granting signs of the hidden victory, and giving to the human words of Christ's messengers the power of God Himself. By the Spirit, men of all nations and tongues are brought to acknowledge the mighty works of God in Christ, and this not only in a kind of symbolic foretaste on the day of Pentecost, but in fullness of realisation through the apostolic witness in all lands. It is the Spirit who gives Christ's people the word to speak when they are brought before kings and governors for His sake. It is the Spirit who grants signs and wonders to accompany the ministry of the apostles, as that of Jesus Himself. It is by the Spirit that the words of the Gospel preaching come with power to the hearers—power to be the actual instrument of God's election (I Thess. 1. 4–5). The gift of the Spirit, itself the sign and foretaste of the age to come, is the means by which the Church is enabled to lead this present age to its consummation, by bringing the Gospel to all nations.

4. Thus the meaning and purpose of this present time, between Christ's coming and His coming again, is that in it the Church is to prosecute its apostolic mission of witness to the world. 'Ye shall receive power, when the Holy Spirit is come upon you: and ye shall be my witnesses both in Jerusalem, and in all Judea and Samaria, and unto the uttermost part of the earth.' The answer to their questions about times and seasons, about the limits of this world's history, is a commission. What has been done for the whole world must be made known to the whole world, so that the whole world may be brought under obedience to the Gospel, and may be healed in the salvation which God has wrought for it. It is for this that the end is held back. The end has been revealed once for all; it must now be made known to all

that all may believe. The decisive victory has been won over the world; the remaining centres of enemy resistance must now be destroyed. That is the meaning of the time still given to us. It is the time for bringing all men and all nations to the obedience of faith. It is for no other purpose that the end is delayed. 'This gospel of the kingdom shall be preached in the whole world for a testimony unto all the nations: and then shall the end come' (Matt. 24. 14). We do not know the times or seasons. But we do know that God has, in the mystery of His mercy, entrusted to His Church a responsibility for making known to all men the salvation which He has wrought. He has made us His ambassadors, beseeching all men to be reconciled to Him. Therefore the answer to our question, 'Lord, how long?', is not a theoretical but a practical one. Ye shall be my witnesses. Go ye unto all the world. The Bible compels us to say, what we would not dare to say for ourselves, that God leads the world to its consummation through the apostolate of the Church.

5. The giving of the commission is followed by Christ's withdrawal from the apostles' sight and by the promise of His coming again. This is interpreted throughout the New Testament in terms of the 110th Psalm. 'The Lord said unto my Lord, Sit thou on my right hand, Till I make thine enemies the footstool of thy feet.' It is because Christ reigns at the Father's side, that the powers of the new age, the powers of the Spirit, are poured forth. He is exalted as head above every power and authority, and yet all things are not yet put in subjection under Him. The issue is not in doubt. He is on the throne. And yet a warfare still goes on in which the Church is His instrument to cast down everything that is exalted against the knowledge of God, to bring all nations to the obedience of faith, and to make all the powers of the world see and acknowledge the manifold wisdom of God (II Cor. 10. 3–5; Rom. 1. 5; Eph. 3. 8–11). The work of the apostles in going from city to city as heralds of the King, not staying to argue with gainsayers, but bearing with them His authority both for peace and for judgment, both for healing and for casting down, all made possible by the living presence of the Holy Spirit, is itself the sign of this hidden reign of Jesus at the Father's right hand. He must reign, as the apostle says, till He hath put all His enemies under His feet.

II

We must now try to see this whole picture of the apostolate of the Church as the meaning of this present time, and show how it is related to the doctrine of the Church as a whole.

1. The salvation of which the Gospel speaks and which is determinative of the nature and function of the Church is—as the very word itself should teach us—a making whole, a healing. It is the summing-up of all things in Christ. It embraces within its scope the restoration of the harmony between man and God, between man and man and between man and nature for which all things were at the first created. It is the restoration to the whole creation of the perfect unity whose creative source and pattern is the unity of perfect love within the being of the triune God. It is in its very essence, universal and cosmic.

In using the word 'universal' I do not intend to exclude the possibility that men may finally be—as the apostle puts it—castaways. To exclude this possibility would obviously be to depart completely from the gravely realistic teaching of the New Testament, with its insistent reminders that there is a broad and easy way leading to destruction and that many go therein. What is intended in the use of the word universal is to emphasise firstly that the nature of the salvation is governed by its source which is a love that reaches out after all men, goes to all lengths to recover one lost sheep, and cares and must ever care for the rebel and the traitor with all the passion of Calvary; secondly, that there can therefore be no private 'salvation', no perfection of joy and rest until the passion of that love is quenched, until He has seen of the travail of His soul and is satisfied. It belongs to the very heart of salvation that we cannot have it in fullness until all for whom it is intended have it together.

It is because this is the nature of salvation, that our experience of it now must have the character of a foretaste, an earnest; that we who have the first fruits must yet groan waiting for our adoption; that we cannot simply be quit of the old Adam and live wholly in the new Adam who is Christ; that we must live still in the flesh by faith, still involved in the old sinful order along with all humanity, while yet at the same time truly involved in the new order of righteousness along with all our brethren, the new humanity in Christ; that we know in our own selves the warfare of flesh and spirit, of bondage and freedom. We cannot enjoy the fullness of salvation until we have it together in the fullness of His body the Church. The new man into which we would fain grow up is a corporate humanity, wherein all the redeemed from every tribe and tongue are made one harmonious whole. Thus the tension which every Christian knows in his own experience between the new man and the old, between the Christ and the old Adam, is—in part at least—the tension of the uncompleted missionary task. We cannot 'grow up in all things into him, which is the head' (Eph. 4. 15), except by going out into the world to make all men one with us in the fullness of His body. The eschatological tension cannot be understood apart from the tension of missionary obligation.

2. We see the same truth by coming at it from another side. It is because the salvation is corporate and cosmic that the manner of its revelation is through a concrete historic event at a particular point of space and time. A message whose essential meaning could be grasped by each individual apart from his relationship with his fellow men and with the rest of the created world could —one may suppose—be revealed at a great number of different places and times. Indeed the only just manner of communication would be—so to speak—a separate communication sent to each individual's address. But a salvation whose very esssence is that it is corporate and cosmic, the restoration of the broken harmony between all men and between man and God and man and nature, must be communicated in a different way. It must be communicated in and by the actual development of a community which embodies—if only in foretaste—the restored harmony of which it speaks. A gospel of reconciliation can only be communicated by a reconciled fellowship. And at the heart of such a community must be the actual historical and geographical centre from which it starts and grows. In other words it will be communicated by the way of election, beginning from one visible centre and spreading always according to the law that each one is chosen in order to be the means of bringing the message of salvation to the next.

3. We may indicate the fundamental interconnection of the eschatological and missionary elements in the Church's nature in yet a third way, by reference to the doctrine of the Holy Spirit. The Holy Spirit is given to us now, while still involved in our solidarity with the old Adam, as the first fruits and earnest of our inheritance in the new. He spans, as it were, the gulf that yet

yawns between the consummation for which we long and our actual life here. By Him we are enabled, in faith, to have fellowship with God the Father whom no man has ever seen, and with God the Son who was manifested to our sight, but whom we do not see and for whose appearing we wait. It is through the Spirit that we are made participants in the victory yet to be revealed. And therefore it is the Spirit who empowers us to go forth to the missionary task, Himself the true witness to Jesus, and the source of those mighty works by which men are enabled to catch a glimpse of the glory to be revealed. Because it is He who gives us the foretaste of the end, it is He who sends us forth to the ends of the earth.

Thus from whichever angle we look at the salvation which Christ has won for us, we see that its implicate is the world mission. The final consummation of God's purpose awaits the fulfilment of the world mission, and this not because of any defect in God's power or grace, but because this belongs to the character of the salvation He has purposed for us. 'The same Lord is Lord of all, and is rich unto all that call upon him: for, Whosoever shall call upon the name of the Lord shall be saved. How then shall they call on him in whom they have not believed? and how shall they believe in him whom they have not heard? and how shall they hear without a preacher? and how shall they preach except they be sent?' (Rom. 10. 12–15). The consummation depends upon sending, upon mission. And the mission is itself the sign of the coming consummation. 'This gospel of the kingdom shall be preached in the whole world for a testimony unto all the nations; and then shall the end come.'

III

This truth about the nature of salvation in Christ must obviously be determinative of the doctrine of the Church. The Church has its existence in relation to the salvation which has been wrought at Christ's coming into the world and is to be consummated at His coming again. Since that consummation concerns the whole world, the Church's existence is in the act of being the bearer of that salvation to the whole world. 'The Church exists by mission as fire exists by burning.'[1] It has its being, so to say, in the mag-

[1] Emil Brunner.

netic field between Christ and the world. Its *koinonia* in Him is a participation in His apostolate to the world. Each Christian congregation is the earnest and foretaste, the *arrabon* of the gathering together of all men of every tribe and tongue around the throne of God and of the Lamb. It is true to its own essential nature only when it takes this fact seriously and therefore treats the world-wide mission of the Church as something which belongs to the very core of its existence as a corporate body. Between the Church militant here on earth, longing for the full possession of that which she has in foretaste, and the consummation for which she longs, the marriage supper of the Lamb, there lies the unfinished missionary task. The first answer to her prayer, 'Come, Lord Jesus,' is His commission—'Go ye into all the world—and lo, I am with you.'

If this be true, then it is high time that its implications for the ecumenical discussion of the nature of the Church were realistically faced. The danger about these discussions is that they may concentrate upon the matters upon which the Churches differ, on which they presumably cannot all be right, and may altogether overlook matters upon which the Churches agree but are quite certainly all wrong. In all the discussions between Catholics and Protestants as to the *esse* and *bene esse* of the Church, I do not remember to have heard the fact seriously faced that a Church which has ceased to be a mission has certainly lost the *esse*, and not merely the *bene esse* of a Church. Yet surely this is so. It is impossible to reconcile with the New Testament the view which seems to be more or less accepted among the majority of Churchmen, that while missionary work is an admirable thing to do, within reasonable limits, it is not something without which the Church simply falls to the ground. We must say bluntly that when the Church ceases to be a mission, then she openly denies the titles by which she is adorned in the New Testament. Apart from actual engagement in the task of being Christ's ambassador to the world, the name 'priests and kings into God' is but a usurped title.

I think it is right to spend a few moments looking at some of the evidences, in the life of the Church, of failure to grasp this truth about the Church's essential nature.

1. The most obvious evidence is the fact that, in the thinking of the vast majority of Christians, the words 'Church' and

'Mission' connote two different kinds of society. The one is conceived to be a society devoted to worship, and the spiritual care
and nurture of its members. It is typically represented by a large
and ancient building. The other is conceived to be a society
devoted to the propagation of the Gospel, passing on its converts
to the safe keeping of 'the Church'. It is not necessary to multiply
illustrations of this separation; or of the absurd situations which
arise from it, both among the older Churches of Christendom
where it originated and among the younger Churches to which
it has been transplanted. Its most vivid symbol to-day is the
parallel existence of two organisations whose personnel largely
overlaps, but which are at present unable to become one—a
World Council of Churches and an International Missionary
Council. The two cannot become one until a very deep and widespread change has taken place in the thinking of the Churches
about their own nature, until they have come to see, and to
express in the ordinary life of the Church, the truth that the
Church has all its treasure entrusted to it for the sake of the world,
and that therefore mission belongs to the very substance of the
Church's life.

2. Less obvious, but equally significant, are the implications of
the ordinary conceptions of missionary strategy which operate
even in Churches which accept the obligation of world-wide
missionary work. It is taken for granted that the missionary
obligation is one that has to be met *after* the needs of the home
have been fully met; that existing gains have to be thoroughly
consolidated before we go further afield; that the world-wide
Church has to be built up with the same sort of prudent calcula-
tion of resources and costs as is expected of any business enterprise.
Must we not contrast this with the sort of strategy that the New
Testament reveals, which seems to be a sort of determination to stake out God's claim to the whole world at once, without
expecting that one area should be fully worked out before the
next is claimed. Thus our Lord forbids His disciples to stay and
argue with those who do not receive them, but tells them to
shake off the dust of their feet for a testimony and go on. And
Paul's missionary planning leaps to the end of the known world,
urging him forward from each field of work to the next, not
when the Church has been fully built up, but when the Gospel
has been fully preached. He carries on his heart always a deep

sorrow concerning the home base. For we must remember that the true home base of the missionary enterprise is the Jews, and that all others can only be called the home base in a secondary sense. Yet he is clear that the right course is not to wait to win the Jews before going on with the Gentile mission, but rather to expect that the conversion of the Gentiles will be the means of life to the Jews. All this is precisely congruous with a conception of the Christian mission which sees it as the sign and instrument of a universal and eschatological salvation, the coming of a kingdom not of this world wherein death shall have been swallowed up in victory. It is the strategy of a kingdom which is God's and not ours.

This same truth has been pressed upon us in a very practical way by the work of Roland Allen in comparing our current missionary methods with those of St. Paul.[1] St. Paul leaves behind him in Ephesus, after only two years of missionary work, a fully established Church provided with its own ministry, able to stand entirely on its own feet. Two centuries would be regarded as a more reasonable period by a missionary of the modern era, and during most of that period the young Church would be treated as a charge on the personal and financial resources of the home base, precluding further advance into new regions. The contrast is startling and becomes more so the more it is examined in detail. Surely it reveals a fundamental defect in our doctrine of the Church. St. Paul is working with a doctrine of the Church which is dominated by the hope of the coming consummation, a consummation which will be wholly the victory of God, but of which the witness of the Church is the sign and instrument, and of which its life is the foretaste. Our missionary methods seem to suggest that we expect an infinitude of time in which the Church on earth can gradually be extended until it covers the whole globe. But the conception of the Church which we tend to reproduce as the fruit of our missionary work is so much a replica of our own, so much that of a fundamentally settled body existing for the sake of its own members rather than of a body of strangers and pilgrims, the sign and instrument of a supernatural and universal salvation to be revealed, that our missionary advance tends to follow the lines of cultural and political expansion, and to falter when that advance stops. Our present methods

Allen: *Missionary Methods, St. Paul's or ours?*

K

show little sign of being able to achieve the enormous new advances which are necessary if the vast unevangelised regions are to be reached.

3. When the eschatological and missionary perspective has been lost from the thinking of the Church, its task comes to be conceived in terms of the rescue of individuals one by one out of this present evil age and their preservation unharmed for the world to come. When this becomes dominant the Church thinks primarily of its duty to care for its own members, and its duty to those outside drops into second place. A conception of pastoral care is developed which seems to assume that the individual believer is primarily a passive recipient of the means of grace which it is the business of the Church to administer. 'The Church', then, comes to mean the paid ministry—and this may and does happen in Churches which claim to repudiate sacerdotalism. There is of course real truth in this picture. The sheep are to be fed by those whom the Lord appoints for the purpose. The faithful steward has to give their due portions to all the household. But when this is taken to be the whole truth, then we must point to other parts of the New Testament which stress the responsibilities of the whole body as a royal priesthood, as the body of Christ in which every member has its proper function. The root of the error lies in the failure to keep in view throughout the *whole* salvation of which the Church is the sign and first-fruit and instrument. If this is done, the Church will be delivered from the tendency to turn in upon itself and will always be turned outwards to the world. It will know itself to be wholly committed in every part to the task of witness to the world in word and in service. It will understand that participation in Christ means participation in His mission to the world, and that therefore true pastoral care, true training in the Christian life, and true use of the means of grace will precisely be in and for the discharge of this missionary task. Speaking in terms of the experience of the village church in India as I know it, this will mean that a newly baptised congregation will not be trained *first* in churchmanship and *then* in missionary responsibility to neighbouring villages. It will receive its training in churchmanship precisely in the discharge of its missionary responsibility. 'Consolidation' will not be the alternative to advance: on the contrary, advance will be the method of consolidation. 'Consolidation' for the

Church of Christ ought not to mean becoming solidly settled on foundations which belong to this world; it should mean accepting and embodying in its life complete solidarity with Him who had not where to lay His head, and agonising with Him for the whole world.

IV

Having said so much regarding the fundamentally missionary nature of the Church, it is, I think, necessary to go on to say a word regarding the danger of over-stressing this truth to the point of defining the Church solely in terms of its missionary function. I have in mind here the work of Dr. J. C. Hoekendijk, who has in recent years most powerfully drawn attention to the danger of an excessively Church-centric conception of the missionary task.[1] Dr. Hoekendijk says: 'The nature of the Church can be sufficiently defined by its function, i.e. its participation in Christ's apostolic ministry.'[2] He repudiates completely the idea of the Church as an end in itself and insists that it must be conceived of solely as instrumental. Even worship is not—if I understand him rightly—a proper function of the Church *in via*. Its apostolate *is* its whole service of God.

I think it is important to protest against this. It is an overemphasis upon the truth with which we are concerned in this lecture, but an overemphasis so excessive as to call for a reminder of the facts to which it fails to do justice.

1. The Church is both a means and an end, because it is a foretaste. It is the community of the Holy Spirit who is the earnest of our inheritance. The Church can only witness to that inheritance because her life is a *real* foretaste of it, a real participation in the life of God Himself. Thus worship and fellowship, offering up praise and adoration to God, receiving His grace, rejoicing in Him, sharing one with another the fruits of the Spirit, and building up one another in love are all essential to the life of the Church. Precisely because the Church is here and now a real foretaste of heaven, she can be the witness and instrument of the

---

[1] See *International Review of Missions*, July 1952, and references there. I am deeply indebted to a study outline prepared by Dr. Hoekendijk for some of the thought of this lecture.

[2] *Op. cit.*, p. 334.

kingdom of heaven. It is precisely because she is not *merely* instrumental that she can be instrumental. This is not a merely theoretical matter, but one of real practical importance. There is a kind of missionary zeal which is forever seeking to win more proselytes but which does not spring from and lead back into a quality of life which seems intrinsically worth having in itself. If we answer the question, 'Why should I become a Christian?' simply by saying 'In order to make others Christians,' we are involved in an infinite regress. The question, 'To what end?', cannot be simply postponed to the *eschaton*.

2. As has been pointed out in previous lectures, the means by which the good news of salvation is propagated must be congruous with the nature of the salvation itself. Salvation is a making whole, a healing of all things in Christ. At each stage of the apostolic task, the Church's task is to reconcile men to God in Christ. She can only do that in so far as she is herself living in Christ, a reconciled fellowship in Him, bound together in the love of the Father. This life in Christ is not merely the instrument of the apostolic mission, it is also its end and purpose. The Church can be instrumental to the divine purpose of salvation only because she is much more than instrumental—because she is in fact herself the body of Christ.

In other words, just as we must insist that a Church which has ceased to be a mission contradicts part of the essential character of the Church, so we must also say that a mission which is not at the same time truly a Church is not a true expression of the divine apostolate. An unchurchly mission is as much a monstrosity as an unmissionary Church. Having entered this caveat, however, against a possible exaggeration, let us re-state the main point with which we are concerned in this lecture, that the very general belief of Christians in most Churches that the Church can exist without being a mission involves a radical contradiction of the truth of the Church's being, and that no recovery of the true wholeness of the Church's nature is possible without a recovery of its radically missionary character.

V

In the previous lecture I tried to show that the Church has to be understood in an eschatological perspective and that only in this perspective is there the possibility of the restoration of its unity. In the present lecture I have sought to show that any eschatology is false which does not carry with it an immediate missionary implication. I shall conclude by reminding you very briefly of the very close connection between the Church's mission and the Church's unity. The connection may be exhibited in a twofold way; firstly, in that unity is in order that the world may believe, and secondly, in that the act of witness sets the Church in the situation in which disunity is seen for what it is.

1. Unity is in order that the world may believe. It has been common in recent years to criticise proposals for union which were advocated on what are called pragmatic grounds. I think that this way of talking needs to be sharply challenged. Certainly a desire for union which subordinated truth to administrative convenience, or which aimed to produce a kind of impression on the world other than the impression which the Holy Spirit produces—the impression of mere size, for instance—would have to be condemned as intrinsically bad. But the indiscriminate use of the word 'pragmatic' as a term of abuse, the suggestion that there is some admixture of lower motives when union is urged for the purpose of making the Church's prosecution of its evangelistic task more effective, is symptomatic of a theology more pagan than Christian. No doubt, as C. S. Lewis has so vividly suggested, the incarnation of the Son of God must have appeared to the pure spirituality of hell a most shocking and degrading episode, but it governs the nature of the Church, which is the continuation of that mission to the world. Certainly, as I have already argued, we must not define the Church *simply* in terms of its mission. The Church, which is the extension to creatures of the life of God Himself, cannot be defined in merely functional terms. But neither can it be described apart from the mission in which it has its being. Our Lord's prayer on the night of His passion binds together indissolubly the Church's relation to God and its relation to the world: He prays for all who believe the apostolic preaching, 'That they may all be one; even as thou, Father, art in me, and I in thee, that they also may be in us: that the world may believe that thou didst send me' (John 17. 21). The Church's unity is the sign and the instrument of the salvation which Christ has wrought and whose final fruition is the summing-up of all things in Christ. In so far as the Church is disunited her life is a direct and public

contradiction of the Gospel, and she is convicted of substituting some partial or sectional message for the good news of the one final and sufficient atoning act wrought in Christ for the whole human race. There is one Lord, one faith, one atoning act, and one baptism by which we are made participants in that atonement. In so far as we, who share that faith and that baptism, prove ourselves unwilling or unable to agree together in one fellowship, we publicly proclaim our disbelief in the sufficiency of that atonement. No one who has shared in the task of seeking to commend Christ to those of other faiths can escape the shame of that denial. It is because we have not truly faced the judgment of the Crucified; because we have not been willing to go down with Him into the place of utter dereliction where He went for us; because we have not allowed the Holy Spirit, who is given only on the far side of Calvary,[1] to have the real mastery of us; because we have clung stubbornly to what we had and have not been willing to cast everything at His feet as we must do when we face one another as fellow-Christians in living and open encounter; because—in short—we have not deeply accepted for ourselves that atonement through death, that we are unable to be made one. And therefore the world does not believe, because it does not see the signs of an atonement so profound and complete that all mankind in all its infinite variety and contrariety can find there its lost unity. To say that the Church must be one in order that the world may believe is to summon one another to a return to the source of the Church's being in Christ himself. As we confront one another—divided by our sundered traditions of speech and practice, yet drawn together by the work of the living Holy Spirit so that we cannot but recognise Christ in one another—we are forced through the crust of our traditions to a fresh contact with the living Christ. As we face the challenge which such encounter addresses to the things we hold most precious, we are compelled to face again the ultimate secret of the Church's being, which is life-through-death in Christ. And when we allow the living Christ to do His atoning work in us, to break down our divisions and to knit us into one, we are by that very fact given a new power to go out to the world to invite all men to share in the atonement which is for all, and in the life of the family here on earth which is the fruit of that atonement, the instrument of

[1] Fison: *The Blessing of the Holy Spirit.*

its furtherance to all nations and all generations, and the sign of its consummation at the end of the world. We cannot be Christ's ambassadors, beseeching all men to be reconciled to God, except we ourselves be willing to be reconciled one to another in Him.

2. One can also exhibit the connection between mission and unity by saying that missionary obedience puts the Church in a situation where its true nature is understood and disunity is seen for what it is. It is no accident that the modern movement for Christian reunion is a byproduct of the modern missionary movement, and that its chief impetus has come from the areas where the Church has been formed by missionary expansion outside the frontiers of the old Christendom. This is more than a matter of perspective, though it is partly so. Evangelistic work places the Church in a situation in which the stark contrast between Christ and no-Christ is constantly being faced. In such a situation other matters necessarily fall into second place. The reality of what Christians have in common is seen to be of an importance far outweighing everything that divides Christians one from another. That profoundly important fact, which most Christians accept in theory, in practice drops out of sight when the missionary task drops out of sight. That is but one example of the corruption which infects a Church which ceases to be a mission. But, as the last sentence indicates, this is more than a matter of proportion. It is a matter of the whole nature and being of the Church. When Christians are engaged in the task of missionary obedience they are in the situation in which the Church is truly the Church. They are actual participators in Christ's apostolate. They participate in His redeeming love for the world, the love which seeks to draw all men to Him. Their bearings are taken, so to say, upon the twin points of Christ's finished work of atonement, and the consummation of that atonement in the drawing together of all men and all nations into one in Christ. In that situation the disunity, which is easily taken for granted among Churches which are not in a missionary situation, becomes literally intolerable. It is felt to contradict the whole nature of the apostolic mission at its heart. It is out of that situation of unbearable self-contradiction that the demand for reunion in the mission field has come.

I do not think that a resolute dealing with our divisions will come except in the context of a quite new acceptance on the part of all the Churches of the obligation to bring the Gospel to every creature; nor do I think that the world will believe that Gospel until it sees more evidence of its power to make us one. These two tasks—mission and unity—must be prosecuted together and in indissoluble relation one with another. We began our discussion by considering its actual context in the life of the Church to-day, and we must end by returning to that context wherein our actual duty is to be done and wherein God meets us in the hard facts of our situation in the world. The unity of the Church will not distil out of a process of purely theological discussion. The religion of the incarnation ought to protect us from such illusions! The so-called 'non-theological factors' in the situation are as much God's concern as the theological, and ought to be as much ours. Our task is, firstly, to call upon the whole Church to a new acceptance of the missionary obligation to bring the whole world to obedience to Christ; secondly, to do everything in our power to extend the area of co-operation between all Christians in the fulfilment of that task, by seeking to draw into the fellowship of the ecumenical movement those who at present stand outside of it to the right and to the left; and thirdly, to press forward unwearyingly with the task of reunion in every place, until all who in every place call upon the name of Jesus are visibly united in one fellowship, the sign and the instrument of God's purpose to sum up all things in Christ, to whom with the Father and the Holy Spirit be all the glory.

INDEX OF BIBLICAL REFERENCES

OLD TESTAMENT

NEW TESTAMENT

153

262.7
N53

7 Day Reserve

3 4711 00222 5490